DISCARD

CONGRESS SHALL
MAKE NO LAW

FREE EXPRESSION IN AMERICA SERIES

CONGRESS SHALL MAKE NO LAW

The First Amendment, Unprotected Expression, and the Supreme Court

David M. O'Brien

ROWMAN & LITTLEFIELD PUBLISHERS, INC.
Lanham • Boulder • New York • Toronto • Plymouth, UK

Published by Rowman & Littlefield Publishers, Inc.
A wholly owned subsidiary of The Rowman & Littlefield Publishing Group, Inc.
4501 Forbes Boulevard, Suite 200, Lanham, Maryland 20706
http://www.rowmanlittlefield.com

Estover Road, Plymouth PL6 7PY, United Kingdom

British Library Cataloguing in Publication Information Available

Library of Congress Cataloging-in-Publication Data

O'Brien, David M.
  Congress shall make no law : the First Amendment, unprotected expression, and the Supreme Court / David M. O'Brien.
    p. cm.— (Free expression in America series)
  Includes bibliographical references and index.
  ISBN 978-1-4422-0510-9 (cloth : alk. paper)
  ISBN 978-1-4422-0512-3 (electronic)
  1. Freedom of speech—United States. 2. Libel and slander—United States. 3. Hate speech—United States. 4. Obscenity (Law)—United States. I. Title.
  KF4772.O27 2010
  342.7308′53—dc22   2010020726

♾ ™ The paper used in this publication meets the minimum requirements of American National Standard for Information Sciences—Permanence of Paper for Printed Library Materials, ANSI/NISO Z39.48-1992.

Printed in the United States of America

For Benjamin, Sara, and Talia

Contents

Foreword

H AS THERE EVER BEEN a categorical command that was categorically honored? Whether the command is on stone tablets or papyrus scrolls or parchment sheets seems not to matter. There are always exceptions. Of course, occasionally there are even exceptions to that categorical claim. Conceptually speaking, this book is about that swirl of exceptions as it moves in one sphere of American constitutional law.

Mindful of such matters, consider the command set out in Article IV, Section 3 of the U.S. Constitution: "[No] new States shall be formed or erected within the Jurisdiction of any other State; nor any State be formed by the Junction of two or more States, or parts of States, without the Consent of the Legislatures of the States concerned as well as of the Congress." That constitutional directive appears pretty straightforward and readily manageable. It seems beyond dispute until one considers the history of West Virginia, which seceded from Virginia during the Civil War and was later admitted into the Union in 1863, though it took another seven years until the Supreme Court settled the controversy.[1] Nonetheless, such precise managerial directives tend, absent crisis or great disagreement, to be honored. But where a command (be it divine or secular) concerns something inherently controversial, in these instances *exceptions* tend in time to qualify such commands by way of judicial interpretation. Case in point: the First Amendment.

"Congress shall make no law . . . abridging the freedom of speech, or of the press."[2] On its face this statement appears unqualified and absolute in its command. This directive might, in the abstract, be thought to require nothing more than a mechanical and straightforward application. Yet, as every student of the Constitution knows, the matter is nowhere near that simple. For even the most mulish of textualists—and the late Justice Hugo L. Black was such a person—have never been categorical in applying that absolutist command concerning freedom of expression. His constitutional mantra—"I believe that 'no law' means no law"[3]—notwithstanding, Black skirted its literal meaning when it suited him.[4] Thus it was with Black, and thus it is today with his interpretive successors. Not surprisingly, it is now constitutional creed that there are so-called well-established exceptions to the First Amendment. Justice Frank Murphy, renowned as a great champion of civil liberties, proffered the most widely quoted maxim concerning this claim. In his opinion for a unanimous Court in *Chaplinsky v. New Hampshire*, Murphy declared:

> Allowing the broadest scope to the language and purpose of the Fourteenth Amendment, it is well understood that the right of free speech is not absolute at all times and under all circumstances. There are certain well-defined and narrowly limited classes of speech, the prevention and punishment of which has never been thought to raise any Constitutional problem. These include the lewd and obscene, the profane, the libelous, and the insulting or "fighting" words—those which by their very utterance inflict injury or tend to incite an immediate breach of the peace. It has been well observed that such utterances are no essential part of any exposition of ideas, and are of such slight social value as a step to truth that any benefit that may be derived from them is clearly outweighed by the social interest in order and morality.[5]

Notably, of the examples of unprotected expression Justice Murphy tendered, some have since come back into the constitutional fold and receive some measure of protection.[6] Moreover, there are other categories of expression, which Murphy did not expressly identify, that are beyond the pale of First Amendment expression—

for example, fraud, trade secrets, copyrighted expression, and child pornography, among others. And former Solicitor General Elena Kagan once urged the Court to create a new First Amendment exception in cases of animal cruelty videos.[7]

It is against that conceptually splattered backdrop that we come to Professor David O'Brien's much-needed original tract concerning exceptions to the absolute command of the First Amendment. In this instructive volume, First Amendment enthusiasts—judges, lawyers, journalists, law students, college students, and laypeople alike—will find a useful and eye-opening account of the ways in which the bulwark of the First Amendment has been breached by judicial doctrine. Or has it? After all, did George Mason, James Madison, and their federal and state constitutional colleagues intend for perjury in court or fraud in the marketplace to be off-limits for lawmakers? Is it reasonably conceivable that they would have believed such forms of expression to be entitled to constitutional protection? Insofar as no sound-minded ratifier would have claimed otherwise, it can be argued that such forms of expression are either not "speech" within the meaning of the First Amendment or are implicit exceptions to its guarantees. Variations on that theme and how it plays out in constitutional adjudication are examined time and again and from different conceptual angles in *Congress Shall Make No Law: The First Amendment, Unprotected Expression, and the Supreme Court*.

"Military men," C. Herman Pritchett once quipped, "are often accused of planning to fight their next war on the lessons taught by the last one."[8] If that is the touchstone, then there is much to learn in the pages of this book. For example, Professor O'Brien's salutary treatment of his subject confirms that if hard cases are not to make for bad law, then exceptions to the constituted law must be allowed. And what are we to think of those exceptions? Do they diminish the coin of our Constitution or do they enrich it? Are they so broad as to imperil freedoms meant to be protected?

In a poignant dissent in a 1949 free speech case, Justice Robert Jackson warned that the Constitution is not a "suicide pact."[9] Abstract absolutes do not work well in perilous contexts. Then again, Professor O'Brien's conceptual spadework likewise reveals what can happen to fundamental principles—sometimes couched in absolute terms to emphasize their importance—when they are reduced to the vagaries of ad hoc balancing. By contrast, judicially created canons such as the "overbreadth" doctrine, strict scrutiny, and the idea of a "preferred position" for the First Amendment are but attempts to mitigate the excesses of balancing. In a concise but helpful way, Professor O'Brien makes this conceptual tug-of-war manifest as he tracks the ever-changing boundary lines of such areas of free speech law as obscenity, indecency, defamation, commercial expression, fighting words, true threats, and student speech.

Another lesson to be gleaned from studying the exceptions to the First Amendment is a point about law and legal reasoning[10] generally. That point demonstrates the challenges of text ruling context, of words governing actions, of absolutes becoming indeterminate, of principles (freedom of speech) warring with consequences (like public or private harms), and of law succumbing to judicial prerogative. By that measure, Professor O'Brien's study offers the reader a treasure trove of information and ideas about how to think about the First Amendment.

This is the latest in the Free Expression in America series, the first volume being Professor Geoffrey Stone's *Top Secret: When Our Government Keeps Us in the Dark* (2007). Professor O'Brien's contribution is a welcome addition to the series, which attempts to buttress the proud edifice of the First Amendment by better informing Americans about it.

Ronald K. L. Collins
University of Washington School of Law

Acknowledgments

THIS BOOK WAS CONCEIVED as part of a project of the First Amendment Center and its book series, Free Expression in America. It would not have been undertaken and completed without the prodding of Ronald K. L. Collins, a former scholar at the center and a professor at the University of Washington School of Law. At the center, I am grateful for the assistance and support of Tiffany Villager and Gene Policinski in the preparation of the manuscript, as well as to Laura Brookover of Georgetown University Law Center, along with anonymous reviewers. At Rowman & Littlefield, Jonathan Sisk was a helpful editor.

1

When "No Law" Doesn't
Mean "No Law"

THE FIRST AMENDMENT DECLARES that "Congress shall make no law . . . abridging the freedom of speech, or of the press." Yet the ink was barely dry after the ratification of the Bill of Rights in 1791 when Congress enacted the Alien and Sedition Acts of 1798. The Sedition Act imposed criminal penalties for "any false, scandalous writing against the government of the United States." It led to twenty-five arrests, seventeen indictments, and ten convictions. Most of them were Jeffersonian-Republican opponents of the Federalists, who were then in power.[1] The laws expired in 1801, after President Thomas Jefferson's 1800 election. But it was not until 163 years later that the Supreme Court took the extraordinary step of declaring them unconstitutional in the landmark ruling on libel in *New York Times Company v. Sullivan* (1964) (discussed in chapter 3).[2]

During the founding period and throughout the nineteenth century, the First Amendment was generally understood in terms of common-law principles and practices. As the most influential eighteenth-century legal commentator Sir William Blackstone observed in his *Commentaries on the Laws of England*:[3]

> The liberty of the press is indeed essential to the nature of a free state; but this consists in laying no *previous* restraints upon publications,

and not in freedom from censure for criminal matter when published. Every freeman has an undoubted right to lay what sentiments he pleases before the public; but if he publishes what is improper, mischievous, or illegal, he must take the consequences of his own temerity.

Blackstone assumed that the Parliament could punish licentious speech and press, and offered no principle or standard for protecting speakers and publishers from subsequent punishment for what they said or published. As late as the dawn of the twentieth century, the Supreme Court maintained that states were generally free to regulate expression, and that "[t]he law is perfectly well settled that the first ten amendments to the Constitution, commonly known as the Bill of Rights, were not intended to lay down any novel principles of government, but simply to embody certain guarantees and immunities which we had inherited from our English ancestors."[4] As Justice Oliver Wendell Holmes (1902–1932) observed, "[T]he main purpose of such constitutional provisions is to 'prevent all such *previous restraints* upon publications as had been practiced by other governments,' and they do not prevent the subsequent punishment of such as may be deemed contrary to the public welfare."[5]

Not until after the Supreme Court in the 1920s and 1930s incorporated the First Amendment's guarantees for freedom of speech and press under the Fourteenth Amendment due process clause,[6] and applied them as restrictions on the states, as well as on Congress and the federal government, did it begin in the early twentieth century to struggle with defining the scope of those protections. Notably, in spite of the First Amendment stipulation that "Congress shall make no law" and silence about state laws governing the exercise of freedom of speech and press, the Court simply announced that the First Amendment applied to the states. In *Gitlow v. New York* (1925),[7] when upholding a state law penalizing the advocacy of criminal anarchy, Justice Edward Sanford (1923–1930) observed, "We may and do assume that freedom of speech and of the press . . . are among the fundamental rights and liberties protected . . . from impairment by the states."

Ad Hoc Balancing versus
First Amendment Absolutism

When the Court initially turned to the task of interpreting the scope of the First Amendment and its applicability to the states, it did so on the basis of common-law principles. A surge of litigation after World War I challenging convictions under the Espionage Act of 1917 and state sedition laws necessitated that the Court develop its own interpretative standards for defining the scope of freedom of speech and press. In *Schenck v. United States* (1919),[8] Justice Holmes initially intimated what would become one of the best known tests: *the clear and present danger test*—"whether the words used are used in such circumstances and are of such a nature as to create a clear and present danger that they will bring about the substantive evils that Congress has a right to prevent." However, Justice Holmes retreated and based his opinion for the Court in *Schenck* on the traditional common-law presumption of the *reasonableness of legislation* and whether the proscribed speech had a *bad tendency*—"whether the statements contained in the [communication] had a natural tendency to produce the forbidden consequences."[9]

Within in a week, in two more unanimous rulings, Justice Holmes again upheld convictions under the Espionage Act on the bad tendency test.[10] But in a fourth case, *Abrams v. United States* (1919),[11] Justice Holmes broke with the majority over the use of the clear and present danger test as an alternative to the bad tendency test. *Abrams* involved the conviction of five individuals under the Espionage Act for distributing leaflets condemning the government's war effort and intervention in Russia, and calling for a general strike of workers in protest. While rejecting the majority's reliance on the bad tendency test, in dissent with Justice Louis Brandeis (1916–1939), Justice Holmes proclaimed, "Only the emergency that makes it immediately dangerous to leave the correction of evil counsels to time warrants making any exception to the sweeping command, 'Congress shall make no law . . . abridging the freedom of speech.'" His dissent in *Abrams* was followed by four other biting dissents and one concurring opinion, establishing the foundations for evolution of this most famous of judicial approaches to the First Amendment.[12]

In the 1920s, the Court continued to hold that the First Amendment did not protect speech and press that might have pernicious effects on society. *Gitlow v. New York* (1925)[13] remains illustrative. There, Justice Sanford reaffirmed the traditional common-law principles governing the punishment of subversive speech:

> Such utterances, by their very nature, involve danger to the public peace and to the security of the State. They threaten breaches of the peace and ultimate revolution. And the immediate danger is none the less real and substantial, because the effect of a given utterance cannot be accurately foreseen. The State cannot reasonably be required to measure the danger from every such utterance in the nice balance of a jeweler's scale. A single revolutionary spark may kindle a fire that, smoldering for a time, may burst into a sweeping and destructive conflagration.

In another famous dissent, in *Gitlow* Justice Holmes reiterated his clear and present danger test. Two years later in *Whitney v. California* (1927),[14] involving the conviction of a Communist under a state syndicalism act, concurring Justice Brandeis endeavored to further sharpen the clear and present danger test. Even in the face of legislation, the First Amendment forbids restrictions short of demonstrating an *imminent clear and present danger*. In Justice Brandeis's words, "Only an emergency can justify repression."

In the following two decades, the clear and present danger test was virtually abandoned. Under the leadership of Chief Justice Charles Evans Hughes (1930–1941), however, the Court began to substantially undermine reliance on the common-law presumption of the reasonableness of legislation and the bad tendency test. In the landmark case of *Near v. Minnesota* (1931),[15] holding that the First Amendment embraced the doctrine of *no prior restraint* on freedom of the press, Chief Justice Hughes indicated that "[t]he conception of the liberty of the press in this country had broadened with the exigencies of the colonial period and with the efforts to secure freedom from oppressive administration."[16] In *Grosjean v. American*

Press Co. (1936), Justice George Sutherland (1921–1938) pressed even further, declaring:[17]

> It is impossible to concede that by the words "freedom of the press" the framers of the amendment intended to adopt merely the narrow view then reflected by the law of England that such freedom consisted only in immunity from previous censorship; for this abuse had then permanently disappeared from English practice. . . . Undoubtedly, the range of a constitutional provision phrased in terms of the common law sometimes may be fixed by recourse to the applicable rules of that law. But the doctrine which justifies such recourse, like other canons of construction, must yield to more compelling reasons whenever they exist.

In addition, a series of rulings extended First Amendment protection to pamphlets and leaflets,[18] peaceful picketing,[19] and subsequently the movies and the cinema,[20] because its guarantees were construed to safeguard "the liberty to discuss publicly and truthfully all matters of public concern without previous restraint or fear of subsequent punishment."[21]

In the 1940s, the clear and present danger test enjoyed a kind of renaissance, buttressed by the Hughes Court's precedents expanding the scope of the First Amendment. The test, though, was also fundamentally transformed during the tenures of Chief Justices Harlan Stone (1941–1946) and Fred Vinson (1946–1953). Justices Holmes and Brandeis had formulated the clear and present danger test as an evidentiary rule for determining the permissibility of applying statutory prohibitions in particular circumstances; they did not purport to establish a standard for reviewing the constitutionality of legislation per se. Moreover, they invoked the test only in cases involving alleged threats to national security. By contrast, the Vinson Court turned the clear and present danger test into a standard for judging both the application and constitutionality per se of statutes. The test also became a basis for reviewing a wide range of restrictions on speech and press, including state laws restricting or prohibiting handbill distributions and solicitations,[22] and requiring compulsory saluting of the American flag,[23] as well as contempt-of-court convictions and individuals' speeches before public assemblies.[24]

As the scope of the First Amendment expanded, some justices pushed for an even more libertarian approach and broader protection for freedom of expression. Chief Justice Stone and Justices Hugo L. Black (1937–1971), William O. Douglas (1939–1975), Frank Murphy (1940–1949), and Wiley Rutledge (1943–1949) contended that the amendment enjoyed a *preferred position*, virtually foreclosing the possibility of upholding any restrictions on free speech and press. As Chief Justice Stone observed, "The First Amendment is not confined to safeguarding freedom of speech and freedom of religion against discriminatory attempts to wipe them out. On the contrary, the Constitution, by virtue of the First and Fourteenth Amendments, has put those freedoms in a preferred position."[25]

Still, the reformulation of the clear and present danger test and articulation of the preferred position approach toward the First Amendment was not without opposition from within the Court. Throughout his twenty-three years on the bench, Justice Felix Frankfurter (1939–1962) criticized his colleagues for their "idle play on words" and "perversion" of the Holmesian-Brandeis formulation of the clear and present danger test, and also ridiculed those embracing a preferred position for devising a "deceptive formula . . . [that] makes for mechanical jurisprudence."[26]

Divisions within the Court were further exacerbated by the political currents in the 1940s and 1950s. Beginning in the early 1940s, political passions again swept the country with dire warnings about Fascism and Communism. In 1940, Congress enacted the Alien Registration Act, or Smith Act, the first federal peacetime sedition act since the Alien and Sedition Acts of 1798. Less restrictive than the Sedition Act, the Smith Act nonetheless made it a crime to advocate or to belong to any organization that advocated the forceful overthrow of the government. Subsequently, Congress required loyalty oaths and statements of non-Communist affiliation from public and private sector employees, with the Labor-Management Relations Act of 1947. The paranoia over Communists continued through the 1950s. Over Democratic President Harry Truman's veto, Congress passed the Internal Security Act of 1950, also known as the McCarran Act, which required members of the Communist Party to register with the U.S. attorney general. Senator Joseph McCarthy's subcommittee and the Special House Committee on Un-American Activities, along with numerous legislative committees, held hearings and investigations of individuals' loyalty.

Bitterly divided, the Court affirmed the constitutionality of both the Smith Act and the McCarran Act in, respectively, *Dennis v. United States* (1951)[27] and *Communist Party of the United States v. Subversive Activities Control Board (SACB)* (1961).[28] *Dennis* remains the watershed case in which the Vinson Court reformulated the clear and present danger test and rendered virtually futile further reliance on the test.[29] In Chief Justice Vinson's hands, the clear and present danger test became a balancing technique for rationalizing restrictions on speech and press.

Writing for a plurality in *Dennis*, Chief Justice Vinson affirmed the convictions of the leaders of the American Communist Party, based on the lower court's opinion written by prominent Judge Learned Hand. Reviewing the evolution of the clear and present danger test since *Schenck*, Judge Hand concluded that it was no more than a balancing technique. But he also ostensibly gave the test greater precision by adding that courts must consider "whether the gravity of the 'evil,' discounted by its improbability, justifies such invasion of free speech as is necessary to avoid the danger." According to Judge Hand and Chief Justice Vinson, restrictions on speech and press were permissible only if they posed a clear and imminent, probable danger, not merely present danger. As refashioned, the clear and present danger test was sharper than Justice Holmes's initial formulation, yet it permitted changing political circumstances to determine the scope of the First Amendment. Turning to international events and the threat of Communism in Europe, Chief Justice Vinson could not imagine "a more probable danger, unless one must wait till the actual eve of hostilities."

Notably, dissenting in *Dennis* Justices Black and Douglas rejected such a balancing of First Amendment freedoms and argued for an *absolutist position*. In Justice Black's words:[30]

> The indictment is that they conspired to organize the Communist Party and to use speech or newspapers and other publications in the future to teach and advocate the forcible overthrow of the

Government. No matter how it is worded, this is a virulent form of prior censorship of speech and press, which I believe the First Amendment forbids. I would hold Section 3 of the Smith Act authorizing this prior restraint unconstitutional on its face and as applied. . . .

So long as this Court exercises the power of judicial review of legislation, I cannot agree that the First Amendment permits us to sustain laws suppressing freedom of speech and press on the basis of Congress' or our own notions of mere "reasonableness." Such a doctrine waters down the First Amendment so that it amounts to little more than an admonition to Congress.

The opinions in *Dennis* underscore the competing interpretative approaches toward the First Amendment in the early and mid-twentieth century. When a second opportunity to interpret the Smith Act arose with *Yates v. United States* (1957),[31] it was anticipated that the result would be different from that in *Dennis*. Oleta Yates and thirteen other second-string functionaries of the Communist Party were prosecuted shortly after *Dennis* was announced. Each was found guilty, fined $10,000, and sentenced to five years in prison. By the time their appeal was granted in 1955, however, Chief Justice Vinson and his three supporters in *Dennis* were off the bench. President Dwight Eisenhower had appointed Earl Warren as chief justice (1953–1969). Justices Stanley Reed (1938–1957), Robert H. Jackson (1941–1954), and Sherman Minton (1949–1951) had been replaced by Justices Charles Whittaker (1957–1962), John M. Harlan (1955–1971), and William J. Brennan Jr. (1956–1990). Still, the Warren Court (with Justices Whittaker and Brennan not participating) declined to strike down the Smith Act in *Yates*. The Court, though, reversed five of the convictions and ordered retrials for the others, setting forth certain conditions for applying the Smith Act that made future convictions exceedingly difficult.

Justice Harlan's opinion for the Court in *Yates* abandoned the clear and present danger test and substituted instead an explicit *balancing approach* on which First Amendment freedoms were weighed against society's right of self-preservation. He claimed that was the essence of *Dennis* in distinguishing between advocacy of abstract doctrines (which receive First Amendment protection) and the advocacy of violence and unlawful action. Two years later, he again provided the voice for a bare majority and reasserted his balancing approach to the First Amendment in *Barenblatt v. United States* (1959).[32]

By the 1960s, the clear and present danger test had evolved into a rhetorical technique, and then gave way to Justice Harlan's explicit balancing of First Amendment freedoms against legislative restrictions. Justice Harlan's balancing approach, however, enjoyed the support only of a bare majority of the Court. In the early 1960s, the Warren Court was split five to four over balancing First Amendment freedoms, with Justice Potter Stewart (1958–1981) as the swing vote. A bare majority, in *Scales v. United States* (1961),[33] upheld the Smith Act's prohibition on membership in subversive organizations and, in *Communist Party of the United States v. Subversives Activities Control Board (SACB)* (1961),[34] the registration requirements for all members of subversive organizations, as established by the Internal Security Act of 1950. In *Scales,* Justice Harlan upheld the membership clause by distinguishing between mere, passive members (the "foolish, deluded, or perhaps merely optimistic") and those knowing, active members whose intent was "to bring about the overthrow of the government as speedily as circumstances would permit." Over the four dissenters' objections that the Court had legitimated "guilt by association," Justice Harlan's opinion for the majority concluded that there was enough evidence that Scales was an "active" member engaged in illegal advocacy. In a second case upholding the SACB, Justice Frankfurter performed the delicate task of writing an opinion for another bare majority. In both cases, Chief Justice Warren and Justices Black, Douglas, and Brennan dissented. One week later, though, Justice Stewart swung over to the dissenters' side to form a majority for reversing the conviction of an individual found in contempt for refusing to answer questions before a subcommittee of the House Committee on Un-American Activities.[35]

Following *Scales,* prosecutions for "subversive activities" under the Smith Act sharply declined. By the mid-1960s, with Democratic President Lyndon B. Johnson's appointments of Justices Abe Fortas (1965–1969) and Thurgood Marshall (1967–1991), there was a solid majority on the Warren Court for striking down portions of the McCarran Act. Because Congress refused to appropriate funds, the

SACB was finally shut down in 1973. A year later, the Special House Committee on Un-American Activities was abolished and its duties transferred to the House Judicial Committee.

In Chief Justice Earl Warren's last term, the Court handed down a brief *per curiam* opinion in *Brandenburg v. Ohio* (1969),[36] finally laying to rest the long line of cases upholding convictions for so-called subversive speech and activities advocating unpopular political doctrines.[37] Provocative and offensive expression of political views may be punished, the Court held, only in circumstances that amount to a call for "imminent lawless action," not merely the advocacy of unlawful and offensive action. In brief concurring opinions, Justices Black and Douglas gave their final requiem for the clear and present danger test and continued to maintain that the First Amendment is absolute: "no law" means "no law."

In short, during the tumultuous first half of the twentieth century the justices were bitterly divided over rival interpretative approaches to the First Amendment, how deferential the Court should be to legislative majorities, what standards should guide the Court's line-drawing, why should freedom of speech and press be valued and protected, and what was the role of the Court in a constitutional democracy. On the one hand, in and out of the Court, there were defenders of balancing First Amendment freedoms, whether under the clear and present danger test or ad hoc balancing. On the other hand, there were defenders of an absolutist approach. As Justice Black summarized his position when giving the James Carpenter Lectures at Columbia University School of Law in 1968:[38]

> My view is, without deviation, without exception, without any ifs, buts, or whereas, that freedom of speech means that government shall not do anything to people, or, in the words of the Magna Carta, move against people, either for the views they have or the views they express or the words they speak or write. Some people would have you believe that this is a very radical position, and maybe it is. But all I am doing is following what to me is the clear wording of the First Amendment that "Congress shall make no law . . . abridging the freedom of speech[,] or of the press."

These two positions—*balancing* and *absolutism*—largely defined the debate over First Amendment freedoms, but neither was unproblematic. Ad hoc balancing was widely criticized within and without the Court for three main reasons: (1) it was ambiguous and unpredictable in application; (2) it failed to establish a constitutional standard for adjudicating claims in a principled fashion; and (3) it tended to legitimate restrictions on speech and press because First Amendment claims were construed as simply private interests to be juxtaposed with public interests in preventing perceived harms to society's self-preservation and punishing licentiousness.[39] However, absolutism appeared too starkly countermajoritarian and too non-deferential to legislative majorities and community interests in punishing perceived harms—harms both public and private.

Definitional Balancing: Categories of Unprotected Speech

As a result, instead of ad hoc balancing or First Amendment absolutism, the Court gradually evolved a *principled* or *definitional balancing* approach to the First Amendment. In other words, as a kind of pragmatic constitutional compromise the Court gradually defined certain *categories* of speech as protected or unprotected per se. The Court's categorical approach or "two-level theory"[40] of the First Amendment was initially suggested by Justice Murphy, when writing for a unanimous Court in *Chaplinsky v. New Hampshire* (1942).[41] There, the Court upheld the conviction under a statute forbidding the use of offensive or disruptive language in public. Writing for the Court, Justice Murphy held that the First Amendment provides no protection for language that is "no essential part of any exposition of ideas." Certain categories of speech—disruptive or fighting words, the obscene, and defamatory speech—were deemed to have minimal, if any, social value and therefore not worthy of constitutional protection. In Justice Murphy's words:

> There are certain well-defined and narrowly limited classes of speech, the prevention and punishment of which has never been thought to raise any constitutional problem. These include the lewd and the obscene, the profane, the libelous, and the insulting or "fighting

words"—those which by their very utterance inflict injury or tend to incite an immediate breach of the peace. It has been observed that such utterances are no essential part of any exposition of ideas, and are of such slight social value as a step to truth that any benefit that may be derived from them is clearly outweighed by the social interest in law and order.

Justice Murphy thus implied a categorical approach or two-level theory of the First Amendment: the amendment safeguards communications that have political and social value, but not certain categories of unprotected speech that cause (public and/or private) harm and are "clearly outweighed by the social interest in order and morality."

To be sure, there are other areas of expression that do not receive First Amendment protection. But they are not categorically constitutionally unprotected. There is no protection, for example, for perjury, plagiarism, contempt of court, fraud and false advertising, insider trading and price fixing, trademark infringements, antitrust,[42] and copyright,[43] or for harassment in the workplace.[44] The Court has also recognized restrictions on prisoners' communications,[45] government employees' speech[46]—particularly pertaining to military secrets—and government-funded expression,[47] along with students' rights,[48] as well as upheld limitations to protect captive audiences.[49] In addition, the Court has upheld "reasonable time, place, and manner"[50] and noise[51] regulations on expression.

Moreover, definitional balancing proved no less problematic than ad hoc balancing or absolutism, since the Court had to define with some precision the categories of and the standards for determining unprotected speech (obscenity, defamatory and commercial speech, as well as fighting words).[52] As Justice John Paul Stevens (1975–2010), concurring in *R. A. V. v. City of St. Paul, Minnesota* (1992),[53] striking down "hate speech" laws, observed:

[M]y colleagues today wrestle with two broad principles: first, that "certain categories of expression [including "fighting words"] are not within the area of constitutionally protected speech;" and second, that "content-based regulations of [expression] are presumptively invalid." Although in past opinions the Court has repeated both of these maxims, it has—quite rightly—adhered to neither with the absolutism suggested. . . . I believe our decisions establish a more complex and subtle analysis, one that considers the content and context of the regulated speech, and the nature and scope of the restriction on speech.

In other words, a categorical or definitional balancing approach defines the contemporary Court's basic framework for First Amendment protected and unprotected expression. But within each category the Court has balanced freedom of expression and perceived harms—harms both public and private—based on the *context* and medium of expression.[54]

Conclusion

The following chapters analyze the Court's defining certain categories of expression—the obscene, the defamatory, commercial, and fighting words or disruptive expression—as constitutionally unprotected in various contexts. In doing so, they put into bold relief the larger issues of what kinds of expression should (and should not) receive First Amendment protection. And why does freedom of expression matter? (1) Is it because freedom of expression has an *instrumental* value in promoting and maintaining democracy and self-governance? (2) Is it because freedom of expression has *intrinsic value* and is essential to individual self-expression and self-determination? (3) Is it because, as Justice Holmes argued, the best test of truth is determined by "the marketplace of ideas"? Or when should community moral values—local, state, or national—override the marketplace of ideas and accepted public discourse outweigh dissenting opinions or individual attempts to deconstruct public discourse? Finally, (4) Is it because once expression is regulated, censored, and punished, the proverbial "slippery slope" of governmental censorship becomes wide open?

The following chapters address those and other controversies over judicial line-drawing within the Court's categorical or definitional balancing of First Amendment freedoms against perceived public and private harms in a wide range of contexts and means of communication.

2

Obscenity, Pornography, and Indecent Expression

T HE PROBLEM OF DEFINING and dealing with obscenity, pornography, and indecent or other offensive speech remains a continuing controversy in the constitutional politics of interpreting and applying the First Amendment. The Supreme Court, in maintaining that obscenity, pornography, and some indecent expression falls outside the scope of First Amendment protection, continues to pose vexing definitional problems presented in a variety of contexts by its own line-drawing. So too, as the Court's composition changed and new technology developed, the tests and boundaries that define obscenity, along with other forms of constitutionally unprotected indecent and offensive speech, have evolved.

Defining Obscenity and Pornography

From the late nineteenth into the twentieth century, federal courts upheld congressional and state power to suppress allegedly obscene materials by applying the extremely restrictive English common-law test set forth in *Regina v. Hicklin* (1868).[1] The so-called *Hicklin* test was "whether the tendency of the matter charged as obscenity is to deprive and corrupt those whose minds are open to such immoral influences and into whose hands a publication of this sort might fall." Under that test books by Balzac, Flaubert, James Joyce, D. H. Lawrence, and Arthur Miller were banned based on isolated passages and the harmful influence they might have on the weakest members of society (children and the mentally disturbed). As Justice Felix Frankfurter was moved to observe, "the incidence of this standard is to reduce the adult population of [the country] to reading only what is fit for children."[2]

Not until *Roth v. United States* and its companion case *Alberts v. California* (1957)[3] was the *Hicklin* test finally repudiated. There, with Justices Black, Douglas, and Harlan in dissent over holding that obscenity is "utterly without redeeming social value" and without First Amendment protection, Justice Brennan proposed a constitutional test for obscenity: "whether to the average person, applying contemporary community standards, the dominant theme of the material taken as a whole appeals to the prurient interests." The dissenters countered, though, that the *Roth* test was problematic. Who is an "average person"? What are "contemporary community standards"? How and where are those standards to be determined? And, finally, what is "prurient interest"?

The Warren Court subsequently expanded the *Roth* test in three other important rulings. In *Kingsley International Corporation v. Regents of the University of New York* (1959),[4] overturning the denial of a license to exhibit the movie *Lady Chatterley's Lover*, Justice Potter Stewart (1958–1981) held that books and films could not be banned for "thematic obscenity"—dealing primarily with sexual themes. In *Manual Enterprises, Inc. v. Day* (1962),[5] Justice Harlan interpreted the "prurient interest" element of *Roth* to require that materials appeal to "prurient interests" in a "patently offensive way." Again writing for the Court in *Jacobellis v. State of Ohio* (1964),[6] Justice Brennan reversed the convictions of the makers and distributors of a film, *The Lovers*, and added to the *Roth* test the requirement that a book or film must be shown to lack "redeeming social importance" according to "national contemporary standards." Finally, in *A Book Named "John Cleland's Memoirs of a Woman of Pleasure" v. Massachusetts* (1966),[7] Justice Brennan combined all three of the above requirements in holding that obscene materials were excluded from First Amendment protection only if they fail all three tests—that is, they (1) have a prurient interest that (2) appeals in a patently offensive way and (3) lack social redeeming value.

As a result of the Warren Court's rulings, basically only hard-core pornography fell outside of the scope of protected speech. The Court's rulings encouraged the proliferation of sexually oriented publications during the 1960s, the decade of the "sexual revolution," and elevated pornography to an issue in national politics. The Warren Court in turn responded to the increased legislation and law enforcement efforts to control the "explosion" in the dissemination of sexually oriented and pornographic materials. The Court, for instance, upheld the conviction of Ralph Ginzburg for pandering by advertising the sale and mailing of his magazine *Eros* from such places as Middlesex, New Jersey; Blue Balls, Montana; and Intercourse, Pennsylvania.[8] Selective prosecutions and bans on the sales of sexually oriented magazines deemed to be harmful to minors were also upheld in *Ginsberg v. New York* (1968),[9] sustaining the conviction of Sam Ginsberg for selling two "girlie" magazines to a sixteen-year-old boy. In addition, permit systems and local censorship boards for screening sexually oriented films were approved as long as they afforded the film's distributors due process and abided by the Court's standards for determining what is obscene.[10]

Still, even in Chief Justice Warren's last term, the Court stood by its expansive reading of the First Amendment. *Stanley v. Georgia* (1969)[11] struck down a statute prohibiting the possession of obscene materials, even in an individual's own house. As Justice Marshall put it in his opinion for the Court, "Whatever may be the justifications for other statutes regulating obscenity, we do not think they reach into the privacy of one's home."

A year after *Stanley*, however, Republican President Richard Nixon's first appointee, Chief Justice Warren E. Burger (1969–1986), came to the Court, followed by the appointment of Justice Harry A. Blackmun (1970–1994). Already critical of the Warren Court's rulings on obscenity as too permissive, Chief Justice Burger quickly tried to persuade his colleagues that the *Roth* line of rulings should be reconsidered. Initially unsuccessful, he was forced to voice his disagreement in dissenting opinions, questioning the propriety of "the national community standard" for obscenity and criticizing the

Court for becoming a "super-censorship board."[12] By 1973, though, Nixon's last two appointees, Justices Lewis F. Powell (1972–1987) and William Rehnquist (1972–2005), were on the Court. And Chief Justice Burger finally commanded a bare majority to agree on a new test for obscenity, ostensibly giving states and localities greater flexibility and control over sexually oriented materials.

In *Miller v. California* (1973),[13] Chief Justice Burger set out more concrete rules for obscenity prosecutions. While maintaining the "prurient interest" test, he redefined it as "whether the work depicts or describes, in a patently offensive way sexual conduct specifically defined by state law," thus inviting states to precisely define obscenity in legislation. Chief Justice Burger also rejected as too broad the "utterly without redeeming social value" test and devised his own more precise test—"whether the work, taken as a whole, lacks serious literary, artistic, political or scientific value." Finally, the "contemporary community standards" test was reinterpreted to mean local, not national, standards.

Sixty companion cases coming down on a five-to-four vote with *Miller* buttressed the Burger Court's ostensibly renewed deference to states and localities in controlling sexually oriented materials. *Paris Adult Theatre I v. Slaton* (1973),[14] for instance, limited the ruling in *Stanley v. Georgia* by upholding state regulation of "adult movie" houses. Prior to *Paris Adult Theatre I*, the Court had held that the First Amendment and the right of privacy did not preclude searches of luggage for obscene materials by U.S. customs officials at airports,[15] but *Stanley v. Georgia* stood for the First Amendment right to possess obscenity in one's home. Subsequently, the Court held that an individual does not have a First Amendment or privacy right to purchase obscene materials.[16]

The most troubling problems with *Miller* arose because obscenity prosecutions under the ruling turned ostensibly on varying local community standards. At the federal level this allowed prosecutors to "forum shop"; that is, they could initiate prosecutions in a district court in a geographical area with the most restrictive community standards. The Court, however, declined to review that practice. For example, the Court refused to hear challenges to obscenity prosecutions in Louisiana for materials produced in California and mailed to New York, but which passed through (and were seized) in Louisiana.[17] At the state level, materials deemed obscene in one state might not be deemed obscene in another. Consequently, the Court left it to federal appellate courts to resolve the matter—in effect, establishing a national standard notwithstanding that under *Miller*'s provision for "local community standards." The Burger Court thus held that the movie *Carnal Knowledge* was not obscene, despite jury and lower court rulings to the contrary.[18]

The Burger Court and, subsequently, the Rehnquist Court tried to clarify some of the other ambiguous aspects of *Miller*, in holding, for example, that children are not part of the "community," but "sensitive persons" and deviant groups are and should be considered in determining whether sexually oriented materials run afoul of "local community standards."[19] The Court also ruled that *Miller*'s third prong—requiring the showing that a work lacks "serious literary, artistic, political, or scientific value"—be applied based on standards set by a "reasonable person," not "an ordinary person."[20]

Besides trying to clarify the application of *Miller*'s tests for obscenity, the Burger and Rehnquist Courts were more receptive to restrictions on the dissemination of sexually oriented materials. Over First Amendment objections, restrictions on the mailing of obscene materials were upheld,[21] as well as zoning restrictions on "adult book" stores and nude dancing, as further discussed below.

The Special Case of Children

The harms to children of exposure to obscene and allegedly indecent expression have been of special concern to communities, state legislatures, Congress, and the Court. While the Court has largely expanded First Amendment protection for obscenity by narrowing that category of unprotected speech to basically hard-core pornography, child pornography has been recognized as a special case because of the harmful effects on children in its production, possession, and distribution.

In *New York v. Ferber* (1982),[22] the Burger Court upheld New York's ban on child pornography. Paul Ferber, the proprietor of a

Manhattan adult bookstore, sold to an undercover police officer two films almost exclusively showing young boys masturbating. He was arrested, tried, and convicted under New York's law prohibiting anyone from knowingly promoting a sexual performance by a child under the age of sixteen by distributing materials depicting such activities. The New York Court of Appeals, however, overturned the conviction and found the statute overly broad and to run afoul of the First Amendment. The state, thereupon, appealed to the Supreme Court, which reversed the state court's decision.

Writing for a unanimous Court in *New York v. Ferber*, Justice Byron White (1962–1993) upheld the statute on a number of grounds: First and foremost was the state's interest in "safeguarding the physical and psychological well being of a minor." Second, and related, the production of child pornography inexorably involves the sexual abuse of children. Third, the advertising and selling of such material promotes an economic incentive for such an illegal activity. Fourth, the argument that live performances and photographs of children engaged in sexual conduct had any value to society outweighed the harm done to children and was dismissed out of hand. Finally, Justice White emphasized that "classifying child pornography as a category of material outside the protection of the First Amendment is not incompatible with our earlier decisions." In addition, Justice White responded to the concerns of the state court and concurring Justices Brennan and Marshall that the New York statute might be overly broad, observing:

> While the reach of the statute is directed at the hard core of child pornography, the Court of Appeals was understandably concerned that some protected expression, ranging from medical textbooks to pictorials in National Geographic would fall prey to the statute. How often, if ever, it may be necessary to employ children to engage in conduct clearly within the reach of the [statute] in order to produce educational, medical or artistic works cannot be known with certainty. Yet we seriously doubt, and it has not been suggested, that these arguably impermissible applications of the statute amount to more than a tiny fraction of the materials with the statute's reach.

Following the ruling in *New York v. Ferber*, the Rehnquist Court upheld an Ohio statute banning the possession and viewing of child pornography in *Osborne v. Ohio* (1990).[23] However, in *Ashcroft v. Free Speech Coalition* (2002),[24] the Rehnquist Court held that Congress may not make it a crime to create, distribute, or possess "virtual child pornography," generated by computer images of young adults or simulated images, rather than images of actual children.

Ashcroft v. Free Speech Coalition stemmed from a challenge to Congress's enactment of the Child Pornography Prevention Act (CPPA) of 1996, which made it a crime to create, distribute, or possess virtual child pornography. The constitutionality of the law was challenged by the Free Speech Coalition—a coalition of artists, photographers, and adult entertainment businesses. A federal district court upheld the CPPA's provisions, but the Court of Appeals for the Ninth Circuit found that the law violated the First Amendment. President George W. Bush's attorney general, John D. Ashcroft, appealed that decision, and the Supreme Court affirmed the appellate court's decision by a six-and-one-half to two-and-a-half vote. Chief Justice Rehnquist filed a dissent, which Justice Scalia joined, and Justice O'Connor issued a separate opinion in part concurring and dissenting.[25]

Writing for the majority in *Ashcroft v. Free Speech Coalition*, Justice Anthony Kennedy (1988–) struck down the CPPA for several reasons. Distinguishing *New York v. Ferber*, he emphasized that children were not involved in the production of "virtual child porn" produced by computer-generated images and other means, and that "the statute would reach visual depictions, such as movies, even if they have redeeming social value." The CPPA, for example, would "embrace a Renaissance painting, depicting a scene from classical mythology, a 'picture' that 'appears to be, of a minor engaging in sexually explicit conduct.' The statute also would prohibit Hollywood movies, filmed with any child actors, if a jury believes an actor 'appears to be' a minor engaging in 'actual or simulated . . . sexual intercourse.'" Moreover, in the majority's view the CPPA failed the *Miller v. California* test that "the work, taken as a whole, appeals to the prurient interest, is patently offensive in light of community standards, and lacks serious literary, artistic, political, or scientific value."

Subsequently, in *Ashcroft v. American Civil Liberties Union*

(2004),[26] the Rehnquist Court affirmed a lower court order enjoining the enforcement of the Child Online Protection Act (COPA) of
1998. Following the Court's invalidation of the Communications
Decency Act (CDA) of 1996 in *Reno v. American Civil Liberties
Union* (1997)[27] (as discussed later in this chapter), Congress enacted
the COPA, prohibiting any person from "knowingly and with
knowledge of the character of the material, interstate or foreign
commerce by means of the World Wide Web, making any communication for commercial purposes that is available to any minor and
that includes any material that is harmful to minors." Compared
with the CDA, Congress limited COPA's scope in three ways. First,
while the CDA applied to communications over the Internet as a
whole, including e-mail messages, the COPA applied only to material displayed on the Web. Second, unlike the CDA, the COPA cov-
ered only communications made "for commercial purposes." And,
third, whereas the CDA prohibited "indecent" and "patently offensive" communications, the COPA restricted only the narrower category of "material harmful to minors." Drawing on the test for
obscenity set forth in *Miller v. California*, the COPA defined "material that is harmful to minors" as

> any communication, picture, image, graphic image file, article, re-
> cording, writing, or other matter of any kind that is obscene or that—
> (A) the average person, applying contemporary community standards,
> would find, taking the material as a whole and with respect to minors,
> is designed to appeal to, or is designed to pander to, the prurient in-
> terest; (B) depicts, describes, or represents, in a manner patently of-
> fensive with respect to minors, an actual or simulated sexual act, or a
> lewd exhibition of the genitals or post-pubescent female breast; and
> (C) taken as a whole, lacks serious literary, artistic, political, or scien-
> tific value for minors.

For each violation of the statute, a civil penalty of up to $50,000 and
criminal penalties of up to six months in prison could be imposed.

One month before the COPA was scheduled to go into effect, the
American Civil Liberties Union (ACLU) challenged the constitutionality of the law. A federal district court granted a motion for a
preliminary injunction barring the enforcement of the act. Subse-

quently, the district court concluded that the ACLU was likely to establish at trial that the COPA could not withstand strict scrutiny because it had not been shown to be the least restrictive means of preventing minors from accessing harmful materials. Attorney General John Ashcroft appealed that decision, and the Court of Appeals for the Third Circuit affirmed the lower court's decision.

On appeal, in *Ashcroft v. American Civil Liberties Union* (2002),[28] the Court held that the law's use of "community standards" to define what material in cyberspace is "harmful to minors" did not necessarily violate the First Amendment. However, the Court also allowed the law to remain enjoined from going into effect until questions about its impact on free speech were resolved. On remand, the appellate court again affirmed the district court's decision and found that the COPA was not narrowly tailored and was not the least restrictive means of preventing minors from using the Internet to obtain access to harmful materials. Ashcroft appealed that decision, and the Supreme Court affirmed the appellate court by a five-to-four vote. Justice Kennedy delivered the opinion of the Court, holding that the appellate court correctly affirmed the order enjoining the enforcement of the COPA. In the bare majority's view, there were "less restrictive" alternatives to the COPA's restrictions on freedom of expression, such as blocking and filtering software. Chief Justice Rehnquist and Justices Sandra Day O'Connor (1981–2006), Antonin Scalia (1986–), and Stephen Breyer (1994–) dissented. On remand for reconsideration, the Court of Appeals for the Third Circuit struck down the COPA as unconstitutional. And in 2009 under Chief Justice John G. Roberts Jr. (2005–), the Court denied review of an appeal of that decision without issuing an opinion, thereby leaving the lower court's ruling intact.[29]

By contrast, in *United States v. American Library Association* (2003),[30] the Rehnquist Court upheld the Children's Internet Protection Act of 2001 (CIPA), requiring public libraries that provide access to the Internet to install pornography filters in their computers. Congress authorized federal funding for public libraries to acquire and to provide access to the Internet under an E-Rate program in the Telecommunications Act of 1996 and the Library Services and Technology Act (LSTA). In 2001, then, Congress enacted the CIPA, mandating that public libraries may not receive federal funding for providing Internet access unless they install software to block obscene or pornographic images and to prevent minors from accessing such materials. The statute authorizes, but does not require, librarians to unblock Internet sites at the request of adult users. It also neither specifies what kinds of filters libraries should install nor provides standards and procedures for unblocking Internet sites for adult users. The American Library Association and a number of other organizations and individuals challenged the constitutionality of the law.

Writing for the majority in *American Library Association*, Chief Justice Rehnquist upheld the CIPA's requirements, observing that

> because of the vast quantity of material on the Internet and the rapid pace at which it changes, libraries cannot possibly segregate, item by item, all the Internet material that is appropriate for inclusion from all that is not. While a library could limit its Internet collection to just those sites it found worthwhile, it could do so only at the cost of excluding an enormous amount of valuable information that it lacks the capacity to review. Given that trade-off, it is entirely reasonable for public libraries to reject that approach and instead exclude certain categories of content, without making individualized judgments that everything they do make available has requisite and appropriate quality. . . .
>
> Because public libraries' use of Internet filtering software does not violate their patrons' First Amendment rights, CIPA does not induce libraries to violate the Constitution, and is a valid exercise of Congress's spending power. Nor does CIPA impose an unconstitutional condition on public libraries.

Concurring, Justice Kennedy emphasized that the CIPA did not violate the First Amendment because adult patrons could request public libraries to unblock Internet sites. By contrast, Justices Stevens, David H. Souter (1990–2009), and Ruth Bader Ginsburg (1993–) dissented, countering that the CIPA ran afoul of the First Amendment. As Justice Souter pointed out:

> A library that chose to block an adult's Internet access to material harmful to children (and whatever else the undiscriminating filter

might interrupt) would impose a content-based restriction on communication of material in the library's control that an adult could otherwise lawfully see. This would simply be censorship. True, the censorship would not necessarily extend to every adult, for an intending Internet user might convince a librarian that he was a true researcher or had a "lawful purpose" to obtain everything the library's terminal could provide. But as to those who did not qualify for discretionary unblocking, the censorship would be complete and, like all censorship by an agency of the Government, presumptively invalid owing to strict scrutiny in implementing the Free Speech Clause of the First Amendment.

Likewise, the Roberts Court, on a seven-to-two vote in *United States v. Williams* (2008),[31] upheld the Prosecutorial Remedies and Other Tools to end the Exploitation of Children Today Act of 2003 (the PROTECT Act). The PROTECT Act aims at curbing the pandering and proliferation of child pornography on the Internet. The law makes it a federal crime for any person who "knowingly . . . advertises, promotes, distributes, or solicits . . . material or purported material in a manner that reflects the belief, or that intended to cause another to believe, that the material or purported material is, or contains—(1) an obscene or visual depiction of a minor engaging in sexually explicit conduct, or (2) a visual depiction of an actual minor engaging in sexually explicit conduct."

In 2004 Michael Williams signed into an Internet chat room, using a sexually explicit screen name. A Secret Service agent had also signed into the chat room under the moniker "Lisa n Miami." The agent noticed that Williams had posted a message that read: "Dad of toddler has 'good' pics of her an [sic] me for swap of your toddler pics, or live cam." The agent struck up a conversation with Williams, leading to an electronic exchange of nonpornographic pictures of children. Later, Williams messaged that he had photographs of men molesting his four-year-old daughter. Suspicious that "Lisa n Miami" was a law enforcement agent, before proceeding further Williams demanded that the agent produce additional pictures. When he did not, Williams posted the following public message in the chat room: "HERE ROOM; I CAN PUT UPLINK CUZ IM FOR REAL—SHE CANT." Appended to this declaration was a hyperlink that led to seven pictures of actual children, ranging in age from approximately five to fifteen, engaging in sexually explicit conduct and displaying their genitals. The Secret Service then obtained a search warrant for Williams's home, where agents seized two hard drives containing twenty-two images of real children engaged in sexually explicit conduct. Williams was charged with possessing and pandering child pornography under the PROTECT Act.

Writing for the Court in *United States v. Williams*, Justice Scalia held that the PROTECT Act was neither overly broad in violation of the First Amendment nor unconstitutionally vague under the Fifth Amendment due process clause. Justice Souter, joined by Justice Ginsburg in dissent, countered that the law swept too broadly in covering artistic works, such as *Romeo and Juliet* and "virtual child pornography," which the Court had ruled the First Amendment protects in *Ashcroft v. Free Speech Coalition* (2002). In their view the majority's opinion also swept too broadly in penalizing the pandering of actual and simulated child pornography and thus undermined the previous rulings in *Ferber* and *Free Speech Coalition*. Notably, they emphasized that banning child pornography could only be justified based on the actual harms done to children, "not the content of the picture but on the need to foil the exploitation of child subjects."

Finally, in spite of the Court's making a special case of child pornography as unprotected speech, and upholding regulations limiting children's access to obscene, pornographic, and allegedly indecent and other offensive speech, as discussed in the next section, it has upheld First Amendment protection for the disclosure and reporting of the names of minors arrested or who were rape victims.[32] In other words, the harms done to children in the production and distribution of child pornography and those potential harms to children of exposure to pornographic materials have been held to outweigh First Amendment freedoms. But the latter freedoms have been deemed to override the privacy interests and harms to minors arrested or who are victims of crimes in promoting the broader public interest in truthful news gathering and reporting.

Indecency, Profanity, and
Modes of Communication

Besides harms to children, the Supreme Court also weighs harms to captive audiences and the general public when upholding or rejecting First Amendment protection for allegedly indecent and profane expression. It has done so based on the context and means of communication. On the one hand, the Court has struck down laws punishing blasphemy[33] and the public displays of expletives[34] and nudity,[35] and also rejected attempts to regulate indecent or obscene speech on the telephone,[36] in cable and satellite communications,[37] and on the Internet.[38] On the other hand, the Court has upheld regulations on nude dancing in adult businesses,[39] the Federal Communications Commission's (FCC) regulation of indecent speech on broadcast radio and television,[40] and restrictions on the federal government's funding of allegedly indecent artistic works,[41] along with students' speech deemed indecent or offensive.[42]

Cohen v. California (1971)[43] provides, perhaps, the classic illustration of the Court's weighing of First Amendment protection for offensive expression within the context of alleged harms to captive audiences and the general public. Paul Robert Cohen was convicted for violating a section of the California penal code that prohibited "malicious and willfully disturb[ing] the peace or quiet of any neighborhood or person . . . by . . . offensive conduct," and received a sentence of thirty days in jail. Cohen, an opponent of the Vietnam War, wore into the corridor of Los Angeles County Courthouse a jacket bearing the words "Fuck the Draft," but when he went into the courtroom, he removed the jacket. When he emerged back into the corridor, where women and children were present, he was arrested, and charged violating California's law, creating a public nuisance, and invading the privacy of those in the courthouse's corridors who were rendered captive audiences. On appeal his conviction was upheld, but the Supreme Court reversed.

Writing for the Court in *Cohen*, Justice Harlan emphasized that states could not single out and criminalize certain words, because that would invite a slippery slope of impermissible governmental censorship and run afoul of the First Amendment principle of state neutrality with respect to the content of communications. As he famously put it, "one man's vulgarity is another's lyric." As for states' alleged interests in protecting against harms to captive audiences, invasions of their privacy, and promoting the public's interests in combating nuisances, Justice Harlan appeared to endorse a distinction between the alleged harms of offensive expression in the public sphere and the intrusion of such expression into the private sphere—such as homes and apartments. Quoting from *Rowan v. U.S. Post Office Department* (1970),[44] which upheld the right of householders to request the post office to order any mailer to stop sending advertisements that are "erotically arousing," Justice Harlan stressed that "we are often 'captives' outside the sanctuary of the home and subject to objectionable speech." Here, Justice Harlan concluded, "Those in the Los Angeles courthouse could effectively avoid further bombardment of their sensibilities simply by averting their eyes."

Justice Harlan's suggested distinction between the public and private spheres in evaluating the harms of indecent and offensive expression was underscored in *Erznoznik v. City of Jacksonville* (1975)[45] and *Federal Communications Commission v. Pacifica Foundation* (1978).[46] In *Erznoznik*, by a six-to-three vote, Justice Powell held that states and localities may not impose zoning regulations that amount to an absolute ban on public displays of nudity. At issue was a drive-in theater's showing films that included nudity, but were not pornographic, that could be seen from the backyards of some homeowners and by passengers in cars on a nearby road. Justice Powell, however, rejected the state's arguments that the offensive movies invaded the privacy interests of homeowners and drivers and their passengers, and also made them captive audiences. The harms in such a public space were deemed *de minimus* and those offended, who claimed to be a captive audience, could simply avert their eyes.

By contrast, the Court took a different approach in *Pacifica Foundation*, dealing with indecent and offensive language on the airwaves. Satirical humorist George Carlin had a twelve-minute monologue, "Filthy Words," about "the words you couldn't say on the public, ah, airwaves, um, the ones you definitely wouldn't say, ever"—"shit, piss, fuck, cunt, cocksucker, motherfucker, and tits." A New York radio station, owned by Pacifica Foundation, broadcast the "Filthy Words" monologue one afternoon in 1973. A few weeks later John Douglas, who heard the broadcast while driving with his young son, wrote a letter to the Federal Communications Commission (FCC) complaining about the indecent language. The FCC subsequently issued a declaratory order granting the complaint and holding that Pacifica "could have been the subject of administrative sanctions." The FCC did not impose formal sanctions, but stated that the order would be "associated with the station's license file, and in the event that subsequent complaints are received, the Commission will then decide whether it should utilize any of the available sanctions it has been granted by Congress." The FCC characterized the language used by Carlin as "patently offensive," though not necessarily obscene. The FCC also expressed the opinion that it should be regulated by principles analogous to those found in the law of nuisance where the "law generally speaks to channeling behavior more than actually prohibiting it. . . . [T]he concept of 'indecent' is intimately connected with the exposure of children to language that describes, in terms patently offensive as measured by contemporary community standards for the broadcast medium, sexual or excretory activities and organs at times of the day when there is a reasonable risk that children may be in the audience." The U.S. Court of Appeals for the District of Columbia, however, reversed, holding that the First Amendment protects indecent and offensive language that is not obscene.

On appeal, the Court reversed the appellate court's decision by a bare majority. Writing for the Court, Justice Stevens upheld the FCC's power to regulate indecent expression on radio and television broadcasts. He did so on basically four grounds. Justice Stevens emphasized that at issue was the intrusion of indecent and offensive expression on unwilling listeners in the privacy of their homes and cars. Second, within the privacy of their homes and cars, indecent and offensive expression necessarily renders homeowners and drivers captive audiences. Third, Justice Stevens highlighted the broadcast media's influence on children who may be unwittingly exposed to indecent and offensive expression, without the opportunity for parental controls. Finally, Justice Stevens underscored that the broadcast media receives less First Amendment protection than the print media or cable and satellite communications, both because broadcasts are on public airwaves and the latter require a subscription, and also generally permit parental blocking of certain channels and programs.

Dissenting Justices Brennan and Marshall countered that Carlin's monologue was "obviously not an erotic appeal to the prurient interests of children." They would have followed and applied the analysis in *Cohen*, rejecting the claims that unwilling listeners' privacy was invaded and that they were rendered a captive audience. In short, offended listeners could simply turn off the radio with minimal effort.[47] Dissenting Justices Stewart and White, joined also by Justices Brennan and Marshall, underscored that the word "indecent" should properly be read as meaning not "obscene," and Carlin's satire was not "obscene."

The FCC's regulation of indecent and offensive expression on the airwaves has nonetheless been reaffirmed. The Roberts Court revisited the FCC's indecency doctrine—that "material that, in context, depicts or describes sexual or excretory activities or organs in terms patently offensive as measured by contemporary community standards for the broadcast medium."[48] *Federal Communications Commission v. Fox Television Stations* (2009)[49] originated after the FCC reprimanded Fox Television for airing brief expletives by singer Cher in 2002 and Nicole Richie in 2003 at the Billboards Music Awards. In 2004, after Janet Jackson's "wardrobe malfunction" during the Super Bowl performance led to a $550,000 fine against CBS television stations, the FCC adopted the position that even brief, "fleeting" expletives expose networks to sanctions because new technology makes it easier to censor such "indecency." By contrast, Fox and other networks argued that the FCC exceeded its authority when an expletive does not convey a sexual message. The Court of Appeals for the Second Circuit agreed that the FCC's policy was "arbitrary and capricious" under the Administrative Procedure Act and the First Amendment. But the Roberts Court reversed the appellate court's decision.

Writing for a bare majority in *Fox Television Stations*, Justice Scalia upheld the FCC's change in policy on indecent broadcasts under the Administrative Procedure Act, holding that it was not "arbitrary" or "capricious" in sanctioning the broadcasting of fleeting expletives. However, Justice Scalia's majority declined to rule on the constitutionality of the FCC's policy under the First Amendment. Justices Kennedy and Thomas filed concurring opinions. Justices Stevens, Ginsburg, and Breyer filed dissenting opinions; Justice Souter joined the latter's dissent.

Dissenting Justice Stevens, who delivered the opinion in *Pacifica Foundation*, sharply criticized the majority for

> assuming that *Pacifica* endorsed a construction of the term "indecent" that would include any expletive that has a sexual or excretory origin. . . . Our holding was narrow in two critical respects. First, we concluded . . . that the statutory term "indecent" was not limited to material that had prurient appeal and instead included material that was in "nonconformance with accepted standards of morality." Second, we upheld the FCC's adjudication that a 12-minute, expletive-filled monologue by satiric humorist George Carlin was indecent "as broadcast." We did not decide whether an isolated expletive could qualify as indecent. And we certainly did not hold that any word with a sexual or scatological origin, however used, was indecent.

Justice Stevens also emphasized that

> [t]here is a critical distinction between the use of an expletive to describe a sexual or excretory function and the use of such a word for an entirely different purpose, such as to express an emotion. One rests at the core of indecency; the other stands miles apart. As any golfer who has watched his partner shank a short approach knows, it would be absurd to accept the suggestion that the resultant four-letter word uttered on the golf course describes sex or excrement and is therefore indecent.

Notably, though, the Court has nonetheless confined its upholding of governmental regulation of indecent and offensive expression to radio and television broadcasting. A series of rulings have reaffirmed First Amendment protection for allegedly indecent and offensive expression by means of cable and satellite communications, which of course offer viewers and listeners more options to (un)subscribe or block channels and programs.[50]

Moreover, the distinction between the public and the private has become increasingly blurred, as indicated by the Court's differentiation of broadcasting from cable communications, and in the 1970s and 1980s by challenges to exclusionary zoning, as well as in the 1990s by congressional legislation aimed at regulating the Internet.

The Court has confronted First Amendment challenges to regulations of indecent and offensive expression in a number of semipublic/private contexts, in which publicly licensed businesses are open only to willing patrons, such as "adult bookstores" and sexually oriented enterprises like adult nightclubs and theaters. Because its captive audience analysis did not apply in these contexts, the Court upheld local and community restrictions on such adult businesses through exclusionary zoning—zoning restrictions on such establishments—based on their secondary effects—namely, the promotion of public nuisances such as crime, prostitution, and community blight.

In *Young v. American Mini Theatres* (1976),[51] a bare majority upheld the decision of Detroit, Michigan, to bar adult-entertainment businesses from operating within a thousand feet of each other or five hundred feet from a residential area. Writing for the majority and in part a plurality, Justice Stevens found that the harmful secondary effects, like crime and prostitution, associated with such establishments provided a compelling governmental basis for the zoning regulation, and in any event did not impose an absolute ban based on the content of the expression. The Court reaffirmed that ruling and reasoning in *Renton v. Playtime Theatres* (1986), among other decisions.[52]

The Court revisited several times the issue of the harms of secondary effects as a basis for regulating establishments that provide nude dancing and other forms of live sexually oriented entertainment. While the Court suggested that nude dancing might receive some First Amendment protection when sustaining a law prohibiting sexually explicit live entertainment in bars,[53] and upheld a state prohibition on the basis of a state's power to regulate liquor under the

Twenty-first Amendment,[54] the Court struck down a state law prohibiting nude dancers in places of adult-only entertainment.[55]

Barnes v. Glen Theatre (1991),[56] however, went beyond earlier rulings on exclusionary zoning in upholding a state statute prohibiting "public nudity" as applied to totally nude dancers in adult clubs, and the state's requiring dancers to wear G-strings and pasties—in short, requiring seminude dancing.

Writing for a plurality in *Barnes v. Glen Theatre*, Chief Justice Rehnquist held that the restriction was a "reasonable time, place, and manner" regulation—a regulation within the sphere of governmental power that furthers governmental interests unrelated to the suppression of expression per se, and imposing a restriction no greater than necessary.[57] Like the chief justice, disregarding that the statute was applied to an adult club, concurring Justices Scalia and Clarence Thomas (1991–) maintained that the law was a "generally applicable law" barring "public nudity" and expressed society's choices about "immorality" and indecent expression.

The crucial vote in *Barnes* was cast by concurring Justice Souter, who relied on the alleged secondary effects of such adult businesses as presented in *Young* and *Renton*. By contrast, dissenting Justices White, Marshall, Stevens, and Blackmun contended that the application of the state's law was arbitrary and capricious in violation of the First Amendment, and that it discriminated between nudity in "high art," such as operas, and "low art," as in strip clubs.

Shortly after the ruling in *Barnes*, Erie, Pennsylvania, enacted an ordinance barring people to publicly appear in "a state of nudity." Two days after the law went into effect, Pap's A. M., the owner of Kandyland, an adult club that featured totally nude dancing, sought an injunction against its enforcement. A trial court granted the injunction upon finding the ordinance unconstitutional. But a state appellate court reversed and in turn was reversed by the state supreme court, which found that nude dancing was expressive conduct protected by the First Amendment. The state supreme court noted that was the view of eight justices in *Barnes* (counting four members in the majority and the four dissenters), and concluded that *Barnes* provided no clear guidance because the Court's decision was five to four and its opinion commanded only a plurality. The city appealed that decision, and the Supreme Court granted review in *City of Erie v. Pap's A. M.* (2000).[58]

In *Pap's A. M.*, Justice O'Connor upheld the city's ordinance, relying on *Barnes* and the secondary-effects reasoning in *Young* and *Renton*. This time, though, Justice Souter, in part dissenting and concurring, questioned the use of the secondary effects doctrine because Erie had not produced any evidence of such harmful effects, but instead simply relied on the thirty-year-old findings in *Young* and *Renton*.

Dissenting Justices Stevens and Ginsburg were even more sharply critical of the plurality's opinion: "Until now, the 'secondary effects' of commercial enterprises featuring indecent entertainment have justified only the regulation of their location. For the first time, the Court has now held that such effects may justify the total suppression of protected speech. Indeed, the plurality opinion concludes that admittedly trivial advancements of a State's interests may provide the basis for censorship." In addition, they pointed out that requiring dancers to wear G-strings was unlikely to combat any alleged secondary effects of such adult establishments. In sum, the secondary effects of adult entertainment enterprises still applies to localities' exclusionary zoning of such businesses, but the doctrine appears to have a dim future unless localities establish empirical links between commercial adult enterprises and their secondary effects on the community.

In contrast to regulations on indecent and offensive expression on broadcast airways and the exclusionary zoning of adult businesses, the Court has generally held that the First Amendment extends protection to such expression on the Internet. In the watershed ruling on the First Amendment and the Internet in *Reno v. American Civil Liberties Union* (1997),[59] the Court emphasized that the Internet is a unique medium, different from print and broadcast communications. In doing so, the Court again underscored that the public/private distinction is often blurred by semipublic/private modes of communications, and thus does not provide a bright line or clear guidance for weighing the allegedly harmful consequences of indecent and offensive expression against First Amendment guarantees.

At issue in *Reno v. ACLU* was the constitutionality of provisions of the Communications Decency Act of 1996 (CDA). When enacting the CDA, Congress sought to protect minors from harmful material on the Internet. The law, among other things, in Section 223(a) criminalized the "knowing" transmission of "obscene or indecent" messages to any recipient under eighteen years of age. Section 233(d) prohibited the "knowing" sending or displaying to a person under eighteen of any message "that, in context, depicts or describes in terms patently offensive as measured by contemporary community standards, sexual or excretory activities or organs." Affirmative defenses were provided for those who took "good faith . . . effective . . . actions" to restrict access by minors to the prohibited communications, and those who restrict such access by requiring certain designated forms of proof of age, such as a verified credit card or an adult identification number. Following the CDA's enactment, the American Civil Liberties Union (ACLU) and a number of businesses and interest groups filed suit challenging the constitutionality of Sections 223(a) and 223(d). A federal district court entered a preliminary injunction against the enforcement of both provisions and the government appealed.

Writing for the Court, with Chief Justice Rehnquist and Justice O'Connor concurring and dissenting in part, Justice Stevens underscored that the Internet is a unique medium—different from print and broadcast means of communication. Therefore, the Court's analysis and outcome differed from that in *Pacifica Foundation*. In comparison to broadcasting, and more like cable communications, the Internet offers means of parental control and blocking indecent and offensive sites. Moreover, Justice Stevens stressed that the CDA was clearly a content regulation and therefore suspect under the First Amendment. And on examination, the CDA was deemed too vague and overly broad in making it a crime to knowingly put "indecent and obscene" material on the Internet and to send it to minors. Justice Stevens, for example, noted that under the CDA an e-mail about the use of contraceptives from a mother to her first-year college daughter could be criminalized under certain circumstances, such as if the daughter attended a college opposed to premarital sex and contraceptives. Finally, Justice Stevens emphasized that unlike the restrictions upheld in *Ginsburg, Young, Renton*, and *Pacifica*

Foundation, the CDA imposed a fifteen-year criminal penalty for violations of the law, instead of simply imposing fines on such indecent and offensive expression.

Following *Reno v. ACLU* the Court struck down the Child Pornography Prevention Act of 1996[60] (as discussed earlier in this chapter), but upheld the Children's Internet Protection Act of 2001, which requires public libraries that receive federal funding to install pornographic filters on computers that provide public access to the Internet.[61] Also, as previously discussed, the Court upheld the Prosecutorial Remedies and Other Tools to end the Exploitation Children Today Act of 2003 (the PROTECT Act), which aims at curbing the pandering and proliferation of child pornography on the Internet.

Conclusion

The constitutionally unprotected category of obscene and pornographic expression has over the course of the twentieth and twenty-first centuries become narrower, limited primarily to hard-core and child pornography. In that regard, the Court has become more defensive of First Amendment guarantees. At the same time, though, the Court has recognized numerous exceptions to the First Amendment's protections: child pornography is a special case, exclusionary zoning of adult establishments has been upheld, totally nude dancing in adult clubs banned, and indecency regulations enforced against radio and television broadcasting, in contrast to cable, satellite, and Internet communications. As technology further develops, the Court is certain to confront new First Amendment challenges to its line-drawing in different contexts. No less certainly, the Court's responses will turn not on a categorized approach, but rather a highly contextualized, nuanced approach to the circumstances, alleged harms, and modes of communication, as well as on its own changing composition and deference to Congress and the states.

3

Defamation and Related Harms

D EFAMATION OF THE CHARACTER of individuals, groups, and the government may be either oral or in print and visual presentations. Slander is defamation by oral presentation; libel is by print or visual presentation. Libel prosecutions may be either criminal or civil. Criminal prosecutions for libel against harms to the government and groups aim at repairing and maintaining the peace and order of a community. Civil suits for harms to individuals are brought for monetary damages.

In historical perspective, the English common law permitted prosecutions for *seditious libel*—libel of the government and government officials—as did the Alien and Sedition Acts of 1798. But in the landmark libel ruling in *New York Times Co. v. Sullivan* (1964),[1] the Court declared the Sedition Act and seditious libel unconstitutional and inconsistent with the First Amendment.

Some states also provided criminal penalties for *group libel*— attacks on racial, ethnic, and religious groups. In *Beauharnais v. Illinois* (1952),[2] the Court upheld an Illinois law making it unlawful to publish or exhibit any writing or picture portraying the "depravity, criminality, unchastity, or lack of virtue of a class of citizens, of any race, color, creed or religion." Beauharnais, head of the White Circle League, had circulated on the streets of Chicago leaflets containing derogatory statements about black people and urging the police to protect white people from their "rapes, knives, guns, and marijuana."

But dissenting Justice Douglas warned that "Today a white man stands convicted for protesting in unseemly language against our decisions invalidating restrictive covenants. Tomorrow a Negro will be hauled before a court for denouncing lynch law in heated terms."

Indeed, *Beauharnais* was widely criticized for failing to consider the close relationship between group libel and seditious libel, and allowing an important area of public discussion—the role of interest groups in American politics—to fall outside of First Amendment protection. Justice Douglas subsequently commanded a majority to strike down a criminal libel law as unconstitutionally vague.[3] Still, the Court has never expressly overruled *Beauharnais* or the concept of group libel. In fact, the Court has cited *Beauharnais* in support of maintaining that defamation receives no First Amendment protection; *Beauharnais*, for instance, was cited approvingly in *R. A. V. v. City of Saint Paul* (1992),[4] even though the Court struck down St. Paul's hate speech law (as further discussed in chapter 5).

Traditionally, *civil libel* suits have been for two kinds of harms and damages: (1) *compensatory damages* as reimbursement for an individual's actual financial loss resulting from, for example, loss of employment or reputation as a result of being libeled; and (2) *punitive damages* as compensation for mental suffering due to a libelous attack.

The Court also distinguishes between libel of *public officials* or *public figures* and *private individuals*. Awards for libel *by* public officials are virtually impossible to win. Members of Congress enjoy virtually absolute immunity under Article I's speech and debate clause for anything said on the floor or in their official capacity.[5] The Court further extended immunity to all federal administrative officials for statements made within the "outer perimeter" of their official duties.[6]

Public Officials and Public Figures

Not until the landmark ruling in *New York Times Co. v. Sullivan* (1964)[7] did the Court set down a national constitutional standard for determining libel *of* public officials and public figures. L. B. Sullivan, a county commissioner in Montgomery, Alabama, sued the New York Times Company for libel published in a full-page advertisement titled "Heed Their Rising Voices," which appealed for funds for the support of the student movement, "the struggle to get out for the right-to-vote," and the legal defense of Dr. Martin Luther King Jr., the leader of the civil rights movement, against a perjury indictment then pending in Montgomery. Although Sullivan was not named in the ad, the page described with some inaccuracies a police action against student and civil rights protesters at Alabama State College. For example, although black students demonstrated on the steps of the state capitol, they sang the national anthem, not "My Country, 'Tis of Thee." Although nine students were expelled, that was not for leading the demonstration but for demanding service at a lunch counter at the Montgomery court house on another day. In addition, although the county police were deployed near the college campus in large numbers, they did not "ring" the campus and were not called to the campus in connection with the demonstrations on the state capitol steps. Moreover, of the 394 copies of the edition of the *Times* containing the ad circulated in Alabama, only about thirty-five copies were distributed in Montgomery County. Nonetheless, a jury found for Sullivan and awarded him $500,000 in damages.

Prior to the ruling in *Sullivan*, states were free to establish their own standards for libel and there was no national standard. But, in *Sullivan*, Justice Brennan declared that public officials may win libel suits only upon showing "actual malice"—that is, the alleged defamation must be made "with knowledge that it was false or with reckless disregard of whether it was false or not."

The ruling in *Sullivan* proved controversial and made it exceedingly difficult for public officials and public figures to win libel suits. Some critics, following Justices Black and Douglas in their concurring opinion in *Sullivan*, argue that the Court did not go far enough toward safeguarding First Amendment freedoms and predicted problems in applying the test. Other critics, however, counter that the *Sullivan* rule renders public officials defenseless against all but the most vicious attacks. As Justice Fortas once observed, "The First

Amendment does not require that we license shotgun attacks on public officials in virtually unlimited open season. The occupation of public officeholder does not forfeit one's membership in the human race."[8]

Following the decision in *Sullivan*, the Court also confronted the problems in defining who are *public officials* and *public figures* and over whether the actual malice test should apply as well to *private individuals*. Public officials, public figures, and private individuals are not, of course, similarly situated, nor do they have the same resources to counter defamatory expression. The Court, for instance, held that a former ski instructor and county commissioner was a public figure, who had to prove actual malice in a libel suit over reports alleging his involvement in city corruption.[9] A year later in two cases, *Associated Press v. Walker* (1967)[10] and *Curtis Publishing Company v. Butts* (1967),[11] both involving public figures, the Court split five to four, with Chief Justice Warren as the swing vote.

In the *Associated Press* case, Edwin A. Walker, a well-known retired "right-wing" general, sought libel damages for a news report that he personally "took command" of a violent crowd protesting the enrollment of James Meredith, a black student, at the University of Mississippi. Walker claimed to have been libeled as a private individual and won a jury award of $500,000 in compensatory damages and $300,000 in punitive damages. However, the trial judge found no malice in the publication and struck down the latter award, which an appellate court affirmed. The Supreme Court unanimously reversed, but disagreed on the standard that applied. Justices Brennan, Douglas, Black, and White, along with Chief Justice Warren, thought that the actual malice test should apply. But Justices Tom Clark (1949–1967), Stewart, and Fortas joined an opinion by Justice Harlan, allowing public figures (unlike public officials) to recover damages on showing only a "highly unreasonable conduct constituting an extreme departure from the standards of investigation and reporting ordinarily adhered to by responsible publishers."

However, in *Curtis Publishing Company*, Justice Harlan and his three supporters in *Walker* were joined by Chief Justice Warren in upholding Wally Butts's libel award of $460,000 for an article in *The Saturday Evening Post*, alleging that Butts, a coach at the University of Georgia, conspired to rig a football game between his team and the University of Alabama. Although Butts, like Walker, was deemed a public figure, Justice Harlan reasoned that here the publication was not "hot news" and, therefore, his standard of highly unreasonable conduct in the investigation and reporting of the story should apply. Though Chief Justice Warren concurred, he nevertheless agreed with the four dissenters that the actual malice test should apply to both public officials and public figures.

Private Individuals

The Warren Court failed to reach complete agreement on the application of the actual malice test to public figures and, moreover, never found a private individual who was not a public figure.[12] Finally, in *Gertz v. Robert Welch, Inc.* (1974),[13] the Burger Court found a private individual and announced a new libel standard for that category of persons—*private individuals must prove only that a publisher was negligent in failing to exercise normal care in reporting*. Elmer Gertz was a Chicago lawyer hired to sue a policeman by a family whose son had been killed by the officer. The John Birch Society, in its magazine *American Opinion*, claimed that Gertz was a "Leninist" and "Communist-fronter" and that the lawsuit against the policeman was part of a nationwide Communist conspiracy to discredit law enforcement. Gertz sued Robert Welch, publisher of the magazine, for libel in federal district court. That court held for the publisher upon applying the *New York Times v. Sullivan* actual malice rule. Gertz appealed to the Court of Appeals for the Seventh Circuit, which affirmed the lower court's ruling, but the Supreme Court reversed and established the lower standard of negligence in the normal care of reporting, instead of applying the actual malice test for private individuals suing for libel. Furthermore, writing for the Court, Justice Powell ruled that private individuals may sue only for compensatory, but not punitive, damages.

Two years later in *Time, Inc. v. Firestone* (1976),[14] Justice Rehnquist reaffirmed the ruling in *Gertz*, when holding that the former wife of the heir to the fortune of the Firestone Corporation was not a public figure, even though she had held news conferences about her divorce. *Time* magazine mistakenly referred to her as an "adulteress," when the divorce decree did not specifically find that she had committed adultery.[15]

Notably in *Gertz*, Justice Powell emphasized that "Under the First Amendment there is no such thing as a false idea. However pernicious an opinion may seem, we depend for its correction not on the conscience of judges and juries but on the competition of other ideas. But there is no constitutional value in false statements of fact." He thereby suggested that statements of "opinion" might be exempt from state libel laws.

Subsequently, in *Philadelphia Newspapers, Inc. v. Hepps* (1986),[16] the Court held that private individuals bringing libel actions have the burden of showing the falsity of reports or stories that touch on matters of public concern. The majority thus shifted the burden of showing falsity in stories of public concern to the plaintiff; Chief Justice Burger and Justices Stevens, White, and Rehnquist dissented. Maurice Hepps was the principal owner of a corporation franchising "Thrifty" stores, which sold primarily beer, soft drinks, and snacks. The *Philadelphia Inquirer* ran a series of articles linking Hepps to organized crime and alleging that he used those connections to influence state government. Hepps sued the publisher of the *Inquirer* in state court and, after a lengthy trial, the jury found in favor of the newspaper. The jury, however, was instructed by the judge that under Pennsylvania law Hepps bore the burden of proving that the articles were false. Hepps appealed to the Pennsylvania Supreme Court, which reversed the lower court and ordered a new trial. Based on its reading of the ruling in *Gertz* the state supreme court held that the burden of showing the truth of its publications rested with the newspaper. But the U.S. Supreme Court reversed that decision.

However, in *Milkovich v. Lorain Journal Co.* (1990),[17] the Rehnquist Court rejected the implication that the holding in *Gertz* applied to expression of opinions that are ostensibly harmful. Michael Milkovich Sr., a high school wrestling coach, sued a small daily newspaper, owned by the Lorain Journal Company, for an article that asserted that he had lied under oath during an investigation of a melee in the school's gymnasium. The newspaper contended that its sportswriter was merely stating an "opinion" for which under *Gertz* he could not be held liable. Writing for the Court, though, Chief Justice Rehnquist rejected that interpretation of *Gertz*:

[W]e do not think this passage from *Gertz* was intended to create a wholesale defamation exemption for anything that might be labeled "opinion." . . . Not only would such an interpretation be contrary to the tenor and context of the passage, but it would also ignore the fact that expressions of "opinion" may often imply an assertion of objective fact. . . .

If a speaker says, "In my opinion John Jones is a liar," he implies a knowledge of facts which lead to the conclusion that Jones told an untruth. Even if the speaker states the facts upon which he bases his opinion, if those facts are either incorrect or incomplete, or if his assessment of them is erroneous, the statement may still imply a false assertion of fact. Simply couching such statements in terms of opinion does not dispel these implications; and the statement, "In my opinion Jones is a liar," can cause as much damage to reputation as the statement, "Jones is a liar." . . .

Apart from their reliance on the *Gertz dictum*, respondents do not really contend that a statement such as, "In my opinion John Jones is a liar," should be protected by a separate privilege for "opinion" under the First Amendment. But they do contend that in every defamation case the First Amendment mandates an inquiry into whether a statement is "opinion" or "fact," and that only the latter statements may be actionable.

They propose that a number of factors developed by the lower courts (in what we hold was a mistaken reliance on the *Gertz dictum*) be considered in deciding which is which. But we think the "breathing space" which "freedoms of expression require in order to survive," *Hepps*,[18] (quoting the *New York Times*), is adequately secured by existing constitutional doctrine without the creation of an artificial dichotomy between "opinion" and "fact."

Foremost, we think *Hepps* stands for the proposition that a statement on matters of public concern must be provable as false before there can be liability under state defamation law, at least in situations, like the present, where a media defendant is involved.

Thus, unlike the statement, "In my opinion Mayor Jones is a liar," the statement, "In my opinion Mayor Jones shows abysmal ignorance by accepting the teachings of Marx and Lenin," would not be actionable. *Hepps* ensures that a statement of opinion relating to matters of

public concern which does not contain a provably false factual conno-
tation will receive full constitutional protection.

Although agreeing with much of the Court's analysis, dissenting
Justice Brennan, joined by Justice Marshall, rejected its application
to the facts in the case at hand and contended the statements made
about Milkovich were entitled to "full constitutional protection." In
their view:

> [A]s long as it is clear to the reader that he is being offered conjecture
> and not solid information, danger to reputation is one we have chosen
> to tolerate in pursuit of individual liberty and the common quest for
> truth and the vitality of society as a whole.
>
> Readers are as capable of independently evaluating the merits of
> such speculative conclusions as they are of evaluating the merits of
> pure opprobrium. Punishing such conjecture protects reputation only
> at the cost of expunging a genuinely useful mechanism for public de-
> bate.

In other rulings, the Court has made it somewhat easier for public
officials and public figures,[19] while somewhat more difficult for private individuals, to win libel awards. *Herbert v. Lando* (1979),[20] for
example, held that at trial attorneys could probe the editorial process—questioning editors and reporters about why certain facts were
included or excluded in their stories—in order to prove "actual malice"; members of the press have no privilege from testifying in libel
cases and answering questions about editorial prepublication decisions. And, as earlier discussed, in *Philadelphia Newspapers, Inc. v.
Hepps* (1986),[21] a bare majority of the Court agreed that private individuals bringing libel actions have the burden of showing the falsity
in reports or stories that touch on matters of public concern.

Subsequently, in *Masson v. The New Yorker Magazine* (1991),[22] the
Rehnquist Court dealt with the complicated question of whether actual malice may be inferred in a libel suit based on evidence of allegedly fabricated quotations.[23] Jeffrey Masson, a psychologist, had
been hired as the projects director of the Sigmund Freud Archives.
Subsequently, his research led him to challenge Freud's reasons for
abandoning his "seduction theory," a controversial theory about

adult emotional disorders rooted in childhood sexual abuse. His discussion of his research resulted in his dismissal from the archives. A year later Janet Malcolm interviewed Masson about the controversy, compiling more than forty hours of taped interviews. Her two-part article was published in *The New Yorker* and republished as a book. Masson sued Malcolm and *The New Yorker* for defamation. He charged that certain direct quotations were altered or fabricated, and that they seriously damaged his reputation. Malcolm, for instance, quoted him as saying if he had remained at the archives it "would have been a center of scholarship, but it would also have been a place of sex, women, and fun." That quote, however, did not appear in transcripts of the interviews. Nonetheless, a federal district court judge found for Malcolm, and a three-judge panel of the U.S. Court of Appeals for the Ninth Circuit affirmed that decision. The majority held that actual malice could not be inferred if the word changes did not "alter the substantive content" or were "rational interpretations" of Masson's unambiguous statements. Masson appealed that decision, and the Supreme Court reversed the appellate court's decision.

Writing for the Court in *Masson*, Justice Anthony Kennedy (1988–) held that the First Amendment does not provide a shield for writers who fabricate quotations. In short, the actual malice test applies to fabricated or incorrect defamatory quotations. On the other hand, the Court has held that the First Amendment protects parodies of individuals' personalities,[24] though individuals may sue in any jurisdiction in which a publication is sold, thus allowing "forum shopping"—the filing of suits in district courts where it is most likely to have a jury favorable to the plaintiff.[25]

The Confusion of Defamation and Invasion of Privacy

Although the Court established national standards and expanded First Amendment protection for publishers and writers against libel actions in *Sullivan* and *Gertz*, it has refused to recognize the difference between libel actions and suits over invasion of privacy. In tort and common law, individuals may sue for basically four kinds of privacy interests: (1) intrusions into their private affairs, causing mental distress; (2) public disclosure of embarrassing facts damaging to their reputation; (3) publicity placing them in a "false light"; and (4) the appropriation of their name or likeness without their permission.[26]

Significantly, in suits for invasion of privacy, unlike those for libel, truth is no defense. Indeed, that is the basic difference between the two—truth is always a defense against libel, whereas in privacy suits it is the truthful disclosure of private affairs that causes mental suffering and injury to reputation. Nonetheless, in giving priority to First Amendment freedoms, the Court applies its tests for libel in cases involving invasion of privacy as well.

As the Court explained in *Time, Inc. v. Hill* (1967),[27] "We create a risk of serious impairment of the indispensable service of a free press in a free society if we saddle the press with the impossible burden of verifying to a certainty the facts associated with news articles with a person's name, picture, or portrait, particularly as related to nondefamatory matter." In this case, the Hills sued *Life* magazine for a pictorial essay on the opening of a play, *The Desperate Hours*, which was based on the Hill family's experiences as hostages of three escaped convicts. The *Life* account, though, failed to differentiate between the truth and fiction in the play, and the Hills sued for invasion of privacy and portrayal of them in false light. The Court, with only Justice Fortas dissenting, reversed a lower court's award to the Hills on the ground that the opening of the play was a matter of public interest.

Seven years later in *Cantrell v. Forest City Publishing Company* (1974),[28] Margaret Cantrell and her children brought an invasion of privacy suit against the Forest City Publishing Company for a follow-up story on a bridge disaster that a year before had claimed the life of her husband. The story inaccurately portrayed the Cantrells as destitute after the bridge collapsed, and Mrs. Cantrell sued for invasion of privacy and misrepresentation. At trial, the judge instructed the jury to find the publisher liable based on the actual malice test. And on appeal, the Court refused to consider whether states may constitutionally apply more relaxed standards of liability for invasion of privacy than for libel.

Furthermore, in *Cox Broadcasting Corporation v. Cohn* (1975),[29] the Court struck down a privacy statute, making it a misdemeanor to name or identify a rape victim, in a case brought by the father of a deceased rape victim against Cox Broadcasting Corporation for identifying his daughter as a rape victim in a television broadcast. Martin Cohn's seventeen-year-old daughter was raped and died as result of the incident. Subsequently, a television report on the incident and the arrest of six youths charged with her rape and murder identified Cohn's daughter as the victim, based on police reports and other public records. Cohn thereupon sued the owner of the television station, Cox Broadcasting Corporation, under a Georgia privacy statute making it a misdemeanor to broadcast the name or identity of a rape victim. The trial judge rejected the arguments of Cox Broadcasting Corporation that its broadcast was protected under the First and Fourteenth Amendments. On appeal, the state supreme court upheld Georgia's statute as a legitimate limitation on the First Amendment, but the Supreme Court reversed that decision—demonstrating both the premium given to First Amendment freedoms over privacy interests and the Court's confusion of defamation and invasion of privacy.

Finally, by a vote of six to three, the Court also overturned a civil award against a newspaper for truthfully reporting, in violation of a state statute, the name of a rape victim,[30] and also ruled that First Amendment interests override claims against publishers for the intentional infliction of mental distress.[31] However, the Court ruled that the First Amendment does not immunize the news media from a suit brought by a "human cannonball" for appropriation of names or likenesses in media coverage of a stunt that allegedly diminished its value.[32]

Conclusion

In sum, although defamatory expression remains a category of constitutionally unprotected speech, the Court has set national standards and, generally, expanded First Amendment protection for allegedly harmful defamation, especially libel, under *Sullivan* and *Gertz*. At the same time, the Court's jurisprudence conflates harms like that of invasion of privacy with defamation in applying its tests for libel.

4

Commercial Speech

A LTHOUGH A CATEGORY of unprotected First Amendment speech, the Court has gradually moved in the direction of extending greater protection to commercial speech. Commercial speech involves the advertising of goods—such as the price of alcohol, tobacco, and prescription drugs—and services, like the costs of attorney's fees, as well as advertising and speech by corporations and businesses aimed at influencing public policy and public opinion.[1]

Why Is Commercial Speech Unprotected?

That commercial speech is a category of unprotected speech was first suggested (as noted in chapter 1) in *Valentine v. Chrestensen* (1942).[2] There, the Court upheld a New York ordinance prohibiting the distribution of "commercial and business advertising matter." Lewis Chrestensen was convicted under the ordinance for distributing handbills that, on one side, advertised his submarine for which he sold tickets to the public to visit, and, on the other side, printed the First Amendment as a protest against the ordinance. The justices unanimously held that there was no "restraint on the government as respects purely commercial advertising." It remained unclear, though, whether commercial speech was unprotected per se (like obscenity) or simply less protected. And why does commercial speech fall outside of First Amendment protection—was it because of the commercial motive, the fact that the content was deemed harmful to community values, or the method of distribution?

The problems with *Valentine* became more apparent in later cases. In *New York Times v. Sullivan* (1964),[3] Justice Brennan ducked the issue of whether an ad, "Heed Their Rising Voices," which solicited funds in support of Dr. Martin Luther King's legal defense and the civil rights movement, fell under the commercial speech doctrine. Writing for the majority in *Sullivan*, Justice Brennan observed that, unlike Chrestensen's handbill,

> [The *New York Times* ad] communicated information, expressed opinion, recited grievances, protested claimed abuses, and sought financial support on behalf of a movement whose existence and objectives are matters of the highest public interest and concern. . . . That the *Times* was paid for publishing the advertisement is as immaterial in this connection as is the fact that newspapers and books are sold.

In *New York Times v. Sullivan*, Justice Brennan implied that the motive of a publisher might be used to define the scope of First Amendment for commercial speech. But in *Pittsburgh Press v. Pittsburgh Commission on Human Rights* (1973),[4] the Burger Court went in the opposite direction, though suggesting that editorial motives may indeed diminish First Amendment protection for commercial speech. There, the *Pittsburgh Press* was found in violation of an ordinance against discriminatory hiring on the basis of gender, due to its carrying "help-wanted advertisements in gender-designated columns." The publisher contended that the First Amendment protected its editorial judgments: it had a right to decide whether to accept an ad in the first place and, once accepted, where to place it in the newspaper. A majority of the Court, however, with Chief Justice Burger and Justice Douglas dissenting, rejected those arguments. Justice Powell, writing for the majority, found no impairment of editorial freedom, emphasizing that "[t]he advertisements, as embroidered by their placement, signaled that the advertisers were likely to show an illegal sex preference in their hiring decisions."

Extending Protection to Commercial Speech

In *Bigelow v. Virginia* (1975),[5] the Burger Court further limited *Valentine* in holding that the "commercial aspects" and "publisher's motives of financial gain" in advertisements do not "negate all First Amendment guarantees." At issue in *Bigelow* was Virginia's prohibition on the advertising of the availability of abortion services and clinics, even those in other states. The Charlottesville *Virginia Weekly* ran an ad for an abortion clinic in New York, and its director and editor, Jeffrey C. Bigelow, was charged and convicted for violating the state statute. Writing for the Court, Justice Blackmun struck down Virginia's law on the ground that the ad promoted public debate and "conveyed information of potential interest and value to a diverse audience—not only to readers possibly in need of the services offered, but also to those with a general curiosity about, or genuine interest in, the subject matter of the law of another State and its development, and to readers seeking reform in Virginia." Justice Blackmun also emphasized that "[t]he relationship of speech to the marketplace of products or of services does not make it valueless in the marketplace of ideas." In addition to recognizing that commercial speech may serve the public interest, Justice Blackmun noted that the availability of abortion was legal, following the landmark ruling just three years earlier (and after the prosecution of Bigelow) in the landmark ruling in *Roe v. Wade* (1973).[6] Because Virginia could no longer ban abortion services, it could not prohibit advertisements for those services. In other words, the greater power of states to ban an activity includes the lesser power to bar advertisements for that activity.

By contrast, dissenting Justice Rehnquist, joined by Justice White, countered that the content of the *Virginia Weekly*'s ad did not distinguish it for First Amendment protection. In his view, the ad was "no different from an advertisement for a bucket shop operation or a Ponzi scheme which has its headquarters in New York." Justice Rehnquist, in short, here and in later cases championed judicial deference to interests in federalism and states' regulations over First Amendment protection for commercial speech. As he would later hold for a bare majority in *Posadas de Puerto Rico Associates v. Tourism Company of Puerto Rico* (1986),[7] Justice Rehnquist emphasized that the states' greater power to bar an activity includes its lesser power to bar ads for that activity—thereby turning Justice Blackmun's reasoning in *Bigelow* on its head—and appealed for a future majority to renew upholding restrictions on commercial speech over First Amendment challenges.

One year after *Bigelow*, a ban on lawyer advertising of routine legal services was struck down.[8] In the aftermath of that decision the Court could not escape a growing controversy over lawyer advertising and increasing challenges to other restrictions on commercial speech. *In re Primus* (1978),[9] for instance, held that the First Amendment protects lawyers who solicit clients for a nonprofit organization (the American Civil Liberties Union). But in *Ohralik v. Ohio State Bar Association* (1978),[10] the Court upheld disciplining an attorney for "ambulance chasing" and soliciting clients on a contingency basis—that is, if winning the case for the client, the lawyer gets a percentage of the award. Subsequently, the Court reaffirmed First Amendment protection for lawyer advertising so long as it is not misleading,[11] while also ruling that lawyers may not be disciplined for advertising in newspapers contingency-fee services if they disclose the difference between "legal fees" and "costs" (the latter paid by the client regardless of the outcome of a case).[12] In addition, the Court held that direct mail solicitation by attorneys was constitutionally protected commercial speech and that state bar associations may not prevent lawyers from soliciting clients in that way.[13]

Following *Bigelow* and the rulings on lawyer advertising and solicitations, the Court extended First Amendment protection to advertisements for contraceptives,[14] by electrical utilities,[15] for real estate,[16] on billboards,[17] and the distribution of commercial handbills,[18] along with unsolicited mailings[19] and advertising and solicitations for other professionals, such as certified public accountants[20] and pharmacists.[21]

The Court's expansion of First Amendment protection for commercial speech based on a public interest rationale came with strong opposition from Justice (and later Chief Justice) Rehnquist. As Justice Blackmun explained, when overruling *Valentine* in *Virginia State*

Board of Pharmacy v. Virginia Citizen Consumer Council (1976),[22] "So long as we preserve a predominantly free enterprise economy, the allocation of our resources in large measure will be made through numerous private economic decisions. It is a matter of public interest that those decisions in the aggregate, be intelligent and well informed. To this end, the free flow of commercial information is indispensable." But, dissenting from that ruling, Justice Rehnquist retorted, "I cannot distinguish between the public's right to know the price of drugs and its right to know the price of title searches or physical examinations or other professional services for which standardized fees are charged."

Confusion: Less-Protected or Unprotected Speech?

In short, the Burger and Rehnquist Courts remained sharply divided over whether commercial speech was still a category of unprotected speech or simply less protected depending on the context. As Justice Scalia observed, "Our jurisprudence has emphasized that 'commercial speech [enjoys] a limited measure of protection, commensurate with its subordinate position in the scale of First Amendment values,' and is subject to 'modes of regulation that might be impermissible in the realm of noncommercial expression.'"[23]

Nor could the justices agree on a rationale or standard for extending or excluding commercial speech from First Amendment protection. Thus, although extending First Amendment protection to advertising by lawyers, public accountants, and pharmacists, the Court declined to do so to optometrists advertising under trade names,[24] and to other kinds of commercial speech, such as college campus advertising for Tupperware parties,[25] editorial and election advertising,[26] lottery ads,[27] and illegal drug–related ads.[28] In addition, depending on the context the Court either upheld or struck down regulatory restrictions on agricultural advertising,[29] casino advertising,[30] door-to-door solicitations,[31] and political advertising.[32]

With only Justice Rehnquist again dissenting in *Central Hudson Gas & Electric Corp. v. Public Service Commission of New York*

(1980),[33] the Burger Court upheld First Amendment protection for a public utility's promotional ads. In doing so, it set forth an important four-factor test for protecting commercial speech: (1) whether the speech concerns a lawful activity and is lawful; (2) whether the asserted governmental interest in banning the speech is substantial, and, if so, (3) whether the regulation directly advances the government's interests; and (4) whether the regulation is no more extensive than necessary to serve the government's interests.

Dissenting Justice Rehnquist charged the majority in *Central Hudson* with returning to "the bygone era of *Lochner v. New York*, in which it was common practice for this Court to strike down economic regulations adopted by a State based on the Court's own notions of the most appropriate means for the State to implement its considered policies." And he warned that "the Court unlocked a Pandora's Box when it 'elevated' commercial speech to the level of traditional political speech by according it First Amendment protection."

The *Central Hudson* test indeed proved problematic in defining the scope and contexts of First Amendment (un)protection for commercial speech. Sometimes the test was used to uphold regulations governing commercial speech.[34] But other times it was used to extend First Amendment protection to commercial speech.[35] More often, though, the *Central Hudson* four-prong test was simply ignored.

In addition to Justice Rehnquist's criticisms of the Court's ruling in *Central Hudson*, Justice Scalia later dismissed the test and the Court's giving in some but not all cases First Amendment protection to commercial speech. In his words, "Our jurisprudence has emphasized that 'commercial speech [enjoys] a limited measure of protection, commensurate with its subordinate position in the scale of First Amendment values,' and is subject to 'modes of regulation that might be impermissible in the realm of noncommercial expression.'" Moreover, Justice Thomas would jettison entirely the *Central Hudson* test and give "strict scrutiny" to regulations of commercial speech. As Justice Thomas put it in a concurring opinion in *Lorillard Tobacco Company v. Reilly* (2001), "I continue to believe that when the government seeks to restrict truthful speech in order to suppress the ideas it conveys, strict scrutiny is appropriate whether or not the speech in question may be characterized as 'commercial speech.' "[36]

Although Justice Rehnquist failed to carry the Court in *Central Hudson*, he amassed a bare majority in *Posadas de Puerto Rico Associates v. Tourism Company of Puerto Rico* (1986)[37] for upholding a ban on casino gambling advertising. In doing so, the Court seemed to reaffirm that commercial speech was a category of unprotected or lesser-protected speech and that the majority would defer to governmental regulations limiting freedom of commercial speech and press.

Posadas de Puerto Rico Associates and Condado Holiday Inn, operators of a gambling casino, sought a declaratory judgment that Puerto Rico's regulations restricting the advertising of casino gambling to residents of Puerto Rico violated their First Amendment rights. The Puerto Rico Superior Court narrowly construed the statute and upheld its restrictions on the advertising of casino gambling. After another appeal to that court was dismissed, an appeal was made the Supreme Court, which granted review.

Writing for a bare majority in *Posadas*, Justice Rehnquist applied (in spite of his earlier criticisms) the four-prong test laid down in *Central Hudson* in upholding Puerto Rico's ban on ads for casino gambling on the island. In doing so, Justice Rehnquist embraced governmental paternalism—community values and morals—as a basis for curbing commercial speech and limiting First Amendment freedoms. Puerto Rico had, in his view, a "substantial governmental interest" in discouraging the "demand for casino gambling by the residents of Puerto Rico" and in promoting "the health, safety, and welfare of its citizens." In addition, Justice Rehnquist turned Justice Blackmun's major argument in *Bigelow* on its head—namely, if the government may prescribe an activity it may therefore bar advertisements promoting that activity. In Justice Rehnquist's words, "The greater power to completely ban casino gambling necessarily includes the lesser power to ban advertising of casino gambling."

The four dissenters in *Posadas* took strong exception to the majority's analysis and renewed holding that commercial speech receives less protection or is an unprotected category of speech under the First Amendment. As dissenting Justice Brennan, joined by Justices

Marshall and Blackmun, observed, "I see no reason why economic speech should be afforded less protection than other types where, as here, the government seeks to suppress commercial speech in order to deprive consumers of accurate information concerning lawful activity." In a separate dissent also joined by Justices Marshall and Blackmun, Justice Stevens took even stronger exception to the use of the "greater power includes the lesser power" rationale for upholding Puerto Rico's ban. As he put it, "Whether a State may ban all advertising of an activity that it permits but could prohibit—such as gambling, prostitution, or the consumption of marijuana or liquor—is an elegant question of constitutional law. It is not, however, appropriate to address that question in this case because Puerto Rico's rather bizarre restraints on speech are so plainly forbidden by the First Amendment." For Justice Stevens, Puerto Rico's law "blatantly discriminate[d] in its punishment of speech depending on the publication, audience, and words employed" because it permitted advertising for casino gambling on the island in the United States but not in publications published on the island for local residents.

Renewing Protection for Commercial Speech

Shortly after the ruling in *Posadas*, however, a majority reasserted its protection for commercial speech. In *Meyer v. Grant* (1988)[38] the Court struck down a Colorado law prohibiting paid circulators of initiative and referendum petitions, advocating a state constitutional amendment to deregulate trucking. In finding the law to violate the First Amendment, Justice Stevens, writing for a unanimous Court, declared that the state's reliance on Justice Rehnquist's opinion in *Posadas* was misplaced.

Subsequently, the Court continued to expand First Amendment protection for commercial speech. Writing for a unanimous Court in *Rubin v. Coors Brewing Company* (1995),[39] Justice Thomas affirmed a lower court's striking down provisions of a 1935 federal statute imposing labeling restrictions on the alcohol content of malt beverages. Under that law the disclosure of alcohol content was required for distilled spirits and wines, while the alcohol content of beer could appear on billboards but not on bottle labels. The government defended the labeling restriction on the ground that it prevented "strength wars" in advertising the sale of beer. The Court, however, held that government's interest failed the *Central Hudson* test requiring the government's interest in regulating commercial speech to be "substantial" and "not more extensive than is necessary to serve that interest."

A decade after *Posadas* the Court, then, expressly rejected the reasoning and ruling in *Posadas*. In *44 Liquormart v. Rhode Island* (1996),[40] Justice Stevens, writing for a unanimous Court, struck down a state ban on advertising the price of liquor. Notably, Chief Justice Rehnquist now joined the opinion for the Court rejecting his analysis in *Posadas* and limiting First Amendment protection for commercial speech.

Rhode Island had two prohibitions against the advertising of the retail price of alcoholic drinks. The first prohibited "advertising in any manner whatsoever" the price of alcoholic drinks, with the exception of price tags, and the second categorically forbade ads making "reference to the price of any alcoholic beverages." In 1991, complaints from competitors about an ad placed by 44 Liquormart in a newspaper generated enforcement proceedings under the statute. Notably, the ad did not state the price of any alcoholic beverages and, indeed, noted, "State law prohibits advertising of liquor prices." Rather, the ad listed 44 Liquormart's low prices for peanuts, potato chips, and Schweppes mixers, as well as identified various brands of packaged liquor with the word "WOW" in larger letters next to pictures of vodka and rum bottles. After being fined $400 for violating the statute, 44 Liquormart sought a declaratory judgment that the state's restrictions ran afoul of the First Amendment. A federal district court agreed that the advertising ban was unconstitutional because it did not "directly advance" the government's interest in reducing alcohol consumption and was "more extensive than necessary to serve that interest." But a federal appellate court reversed that decision and 44 Liquormart appealed to the Supreme Court, which in turn reversed the appellate court and struck down Rhode Island's statute as unconstitutional.

Writing for the Court in *44 Liquormart*, Justice Stevens swept

broadly in reviewing the history of rulings on First Amendment protection for commercial speech in order to emphasize that *Posadas*
had "erroneously performed the [proper] First Amendment analysis," and that that decision "clearly erred in concluding that it was
'up to the legislature' to choose suppression over a less speech-
restrictive policy." To the contrary, Justice Stevens concluded "that
a state legislature does not have the broad discretion to suppress
truthful, nonmisleading information for paternalistic purposes that
the *Posadas* majority was willing to tolerate." In rejecting paternalist
rationales for limiting commercial speech, Justice Stevens underscored that any "vice" exception to the First Amendment "would be
difficult, if not impossible, to define." And noting that there was no
empirical evidence that bans on ads for alcohol resulted in diminished consumption, he added the following:

> Almost any product that poses some threat to public health or public
> morals might reasonably be characterized by a state legislature as re-
> lating to "vice activity." Such characterization, however, is anomalous
> when applied to products such as alcohol beverages, lottery tickets, or
> playing cards, that may be lawfully purchased on the open market. . . .
> For these reasons, a "vice" label that is unaccompanied by a corre-
> sponding prohibition against the commercial behavior at issue fails to
> provide a principled justification for the regulation of commercial
> speech about that activity.

Furthermore, Justice Stevens expressly dismissed the "syllogism"
that "greater powers include lesser ones":

> Contrary to the assumption made in *Posadas*, we think it quite clear
> that banning speech may sometimes prove far more intrusive than
> banning conduct. As a venerable proverb teaches, it may prove more
> injurious to prevent people from teaching others how to fish than to
> prevent fish from being sold. Similarly, a local ordinance banning bi-
> cycle lessons may curtail freedom far more than one that prohibits
> bicycle riding within city limits. In short, we reject the assumption
> that words are necessarily less vital to freedom than actions, or that
> logic somehow proves that the power to prohibit an activity is neces-
> sarily "greater" than the power to suppress speech about it.

Notably, concurring Justices Scalia and Thomas would have completely jettisoned the *Central Hudson* test and extended First Amendment protection to commercial speech, while concurring Justice O'Connor would have resolved *44 Liquormart* more narrowly by applying the *Central Hudson* test.

The unanimous ruling in *44 Liquormart* signaled and solidified the expanded First Amendment protection for commercial speech in rejecting paternalistic and moralistic arguments for regulating commercial discourse. To be sure, the issue of permitting regulations of commercial speech continues to sharply divide the justices based on the regulatory context presented.

In *Lorillard Tobacco Company v. Reilly* (2001),[41] for instance, Justice O'Connor held for a bare majority that federal regulations of cigarette advertising preempted Massachusetts's regulations of displays for their sales and that the state's regulation of ads for smokeless tobacco products violated the First Amendment. Justices Stevens, Souter, Ginsburg, and Breyer, however, dissented and would have held that Massachusetts's regulations did not run afoul of the First Amendment. Again writing for another bare majority in *Thompson v. Western States Medical Center* (2002),[42] Justice O'Connor struck down a federal restriction on the advertising of "compound drugs," with Chief Justice Rehnquist and Justices Stevens, Ginsburg, and Breyer dissenting.

But in other cases the justices have lined up differently in upholding laws permitting police departments to give access to journalists to arrest records but not to companies for commercial purposes,[43] and so-called government speech under which governmental regulations require producers to contribute to funds for marketing campaigns for their products.[44]

Conclusion

In short, while commercial speech remains a category of constitutionally unprotected or lesser-protected speech under the First Amendment, over the last two decades the Court has expanded protection for commercial speech. The underlying controversies—

controversies over private versus public interests, market forces versus paternalism and community values, and the role of courts versus legislatures in protecting or restricting freedom of speech and press—continue to divide the justices. The Court remains divided, at times, between liberals versus conservatives on the bench, and divided even among conservatives, like former Chief Justice Rehnquist versus Justices Scalia and Thomas. Both liberal and conservative justices have also splintered depending on the case, controversy, or context. Still, the conclusion remains inescapable that commercial speech has attained a higher degree of First Amendment protection and that governmental interests in protecting against perceived public and private harms associated with mass commercial communications are generally subordinate to First Amendment freedoms.

5

"Fighting Words," Provocative and Disruptive Expression

"FIGHTING WORDS" were declared a category of constitutionally unprotected speech in *Chaplinsky v. New Hampshire* (1942),[1] as noted in chapter 1. There, the Court upheld the conviction under a state statute forbidding the use of offensive or disruptive language in public. Walter Chaplinsky, a proselytizing Jehovah's Witness, at the time of his arrest for creating a public disturbance, called the arresting officer "a Goddamned racketeer" and a "damned Fascist." Writing for a unanimous Court, Justice Murphy held that the First Amendment provides no protection for such words because they "are no essential part of any exposition of ideas." As Justice Murphy observed, "[T]he insulting or 'fighting words'—those which by their very utterance inflict injury or tend to incite an immediate breach of the peace . . . [are] clearly outweighed by the social interest in law and order."

Still, although never overruling *Chaplinsky*, the Court has not found another unprotected "fighting word,"[2] even when expressed before hostile audiences.[3] Indeed, the "fighting words" category has been rendered by the Court (though not lower and state courts) a virtually null category.[4] Even an invitation to a brawl appears to be protected. The Court, for example, reversed the conviction of a man who, while being arrested, rather unambiguously invited a fight by calling a police officer a "son-of-a-bitch" and threatening to kill him.[5] The Court also struck down an ordinance prohibiting the cursing of police officers,[6] and invalidated a law that made it unlawful to interfere with a police officer while performing his duties.[7]

The Court extended First Amendment protection to "fighting words" and other provocative and disruptive speech because such offensive speech may convey a political statement, and hence entitled to protection. For instance, in *Watts v. United States* (1969),[8] the Court overturned the conviction of an individual who, at a protest rally against the Vietnam War, shouted, "If they ever make me carry a rifle, the first man I want to get is LBJ [President Lyndon B. Johnson]." The justices agreed (six to three) that the federal statute criminalizing threats against the life of the president must be strictly construed and the statement here was an expression of political views, rather than an actual *true threat*.[9] In addition, the Court extended First Amendment protection to protestors before hostile audiences that allegedly create public disturbances.[10]

Nonetheless, the Court has found other exceptions to First Amendment protection for provocative and disruptive expression, depending on the context, that remains related to the category of constitutionally unprotected "fighting words." It has done so when confronting First Amendment challenges to hate-speech laws and *true threats*, symbolic speech and speech-plus-conduct, as well as restrictions on students' expression. These areas, and how in different contexts the Court has drawn the lines between protected and unprotected expression differently, are the subject of this chapter.

Hate-Speech Laws and "True Threats"

Hate-speech laws—laws that fine or criminalize speech that disparages or arouses anger by intimating others on the basis of race, color, creed, religion, or gender—have been around for a long time. But in the 1980s and 1990s more than thirty states and numerous localities and colleges enacted hate-speech codes. They basically took two forms: (1) some punished hate speech per se, while (2) others provided for enhanced sentences for individuals found guilty of criminal assaults or vandalism, mandating longer prison sentences for those convicted of such crimes when the victim was singled out based on racial, ethnic, religious, or gender bias.

The Court upheld a hate-speech or group-libel law in *Beauharnais v. Illinois* (1952),[11] as discussed in chapter 3. At issue was an Illinois law making it unlawful to criticize or portray the "depravity, criminality, unchastity, or lack of virtue of a class of citizens, of any race, color, creed, or religion." Beauharnais, head of the White Circle League, had circulated leaflets containing derogatory statements about black people and urging police to protect white people from their "rapes, knives, guns, and marijuana."

Although *Beauharnais* has not been overruled,[12] the Court has been more defensive of First Amendment guarantees when confronting challenges to recent hate-speech laws. In *R. A. V. v. City of St. Paul, Minnesota* (1992),[13] the Court unanimously invalidated St. Paul's hate-speech ordinance—making it a crime to place on public or private property a burning cross, swastika, or other symbol likely to arouse "anger, alarm, or resentment in others on the basis of race, color, creed, religion, or gender." Robert A. Viktora, a white teenager, and several other white youths burned a cross made of a broken chair after midnight on the lawn of the only black family in a St. Paul neighborhood. He was later arrested and charged with violating the city's ordinance. A state juvenile court, however, dismissed the complaint on the ground that the ordinance was overly broad and unconstitutional. But the Minnesota Supreme Court reversed on concluding that the ordinance applied only to conduct "outside First Amendment protection." In determining that the ordinance only prohibited "fighting words" or speech that threatens "imminent lawless action," the state supreme court observed, "The burning of a cross is itself an unmistakable symbol of violence and hatred based on virulent notions of racial supremacy." St. Paul did not ban cross burning per se, the court reasoned, "but only those displays that one knows or should know will create anger, alarm or resentment based on racial, ethnic, gender, or religious bias." Robert A. Viktora appealed that ruling to the Supreme Court, and it reversed the state supreme court.

Writing for the Court in *R. A. V.*, Justice Scalia ruled that even within the category of "fighting words" governments may not bar or penalize the expression of some but not other words based on their content. In short, the ordinance was underinclusive. As Justice Scalia explained:

> Displays containing abusive invective, no matter how vicious or severe, are permissible unless they are addressed to one of the specified disfavored topics. Those who wish to use "fighting words" in connection with other ideas—to express hostility, for example, on the basis of political affiliation, union membership, or homosexuality—are not covered. The First Amendment does not permit St. Paul to impose special prohibitions on those speakers who express views on disfavored subjects. In its practical operation, moreover, the ordinance goes even beyond mere content discrimination, to actual viewpoint discrimination. Displays containing some words—odious racial epithets, for example—would be prohibited to proponents of all views. But "fighting words" that do not themselves invoke race, color, creed, religion, or gender—aspersions upon a person's mother, for example—would seemingly be usable ad libitum in the placards of those arguing in favor of racial, color, etc., tolerance and equality, but could not be used by that speaker's opponents.

Yet only Chief Justice Rehnquist and Justices Kennedy, Souter, and Thomas joined Justice Scalia's opinion for the Court. In concurring opinions that read more like dissents, Justices Blackmun, Stevens, O'Connor, and White accused the majority of rewriting First Amendment doctrine. They would have overturned the ordinance as "fatally overbroad because it criminalizes not only unprotected expression but expression protected by the First Amendment."

Despite the unanimity on the result in *R. A. V.*, the fragmentation of the justices contributed to the Court's willingness to revisit the controversy over other hate-speech laws—laws imposing enhanced sentences for hate speech, such as in *Wisconsin v. Mitchell* (1993).[14] Todd Mitchell and several other black men and youths were talking about a scene in the movie *Mississippi Burning*, in which a white man beats a young black man. Later, as the group moved outside to the street, Mitchell asked them, "Do you all feel hyped up to move on some white people?" Shortly thereafter a young white boy appeared on the other side of the street, and as he walked by, Mitchell counted "one, two, three" and said, "There goes a white boy; go get him!"

After rushing the boy, Mitchell and the others beat him unconscious and stole his tennis shoes. Subsequently, Mitchell was convicted of battery, which carried a maximum sentence of two years' imprisonment. But under Wisconsin's hate-speech law an enhanced sentence may be given whenever a defendant "intentionally selects the person against whom the crime . . . is committed . . . because of the race, religion, color, disability, sexual orientation, national origin or ancestry of that person." Accordingly, Mitchell was sentenced to four years' imprisonment. His challenge to the state's law and his conviction was initially unsuccessful, but on appeal the state supreme court agreed that the law violated "the First Amendment directly by punishing what the legislature has deemed to be offensive thought." The Supreme Court, however, reversed and upheld Wisconsin's sentence-enhancing hate-speech law.

Unlike *R. A. V.*, the justices unanimously joined Chief Justice Rehnquist's opinion for the Court, upholding hate-speech laws that mandate longer sentences for individuals convicted of assault or vandalism when the crime was committed and the victim was selected because of racial, religious, gender, or ethnic bias. Chief Justice Rehnquist did so by focusing on Wisconsin's targeting *conduct*, unlike St. Paul's ordinance, which targeted expression per se. Accordingly, the chief justice distinguished *R. A. V.*, observing that

> [n]othing . . . in *R. A. V.* compels a different result here. That case involved a First Amendment challenge to a municipal ordinance prohibiting the use of " 'fighting words' that insult, or provoke violence, 'on the basis of race, color, creed, religion or gender.' " Because the ordinance only proscribed a class of "fighting words" deemed particularly offensive by the city—i.e., those that "contain . . . messages of 'bias-motivated' hatred"—we held that it violated the rule against content-based discrimination. But whereas the ordinance struck down in *R. A. V.* was explicitly directed at expression (i.e., "speech" or "messages"), the statute in this case is aimed at conduct unprotected by the First Amendment.

The Court later revisited the controversy over cross burning in *Virginia v. Black* (2003).[15] As in *Watts v. United States* (1969)[16] (discussed at the outset of this chapter), the Court in *Virginia v. Black* carefully distinguished between political expression and *true threats* or explicit intimidation in cross burning, no less than other forms of provocative and offensive expression.[17]

Virginia v. Black is a complex case because it consolidated two cases involving cross burning in different circumstances. Barry Elton Black led a Ku Klux Klan rally at which a twenty-five-foot cross was burned on private property with the owner's permission, but which was clearly visible to nearby homeowners and motorists on a state road. He was convicted under Virginia's fifty-year-old law making cross burning a crime, and fined $2,500. In a separate case, Richard J. Elliott and Jonathan O'Mara burned a cross in the yard of James Jubilee, an African American, because they were angry with him. Both were convicted and sentenced to ninety days in jail and fined $2,500 each. On appeal, the Virginia Supreme Court overturned their convictions and struck down the state's law in holding that it ran afoul of the First Amendment's guarantee for freedom of expression.

On appeal of the state supreme court's decision, Justice O'Connor's opinion for the Court commanded only a plurality, but by a six-to-three vote held that a properly drafted law punishing cross burning would survive First Amendment challenge. Justice O'Connor's opinion, joined by Chief Justice Rehnquist and Justices Stevens and Breyer, held that states may make it a crime to burn a cross because it is "a particularly virulent form of intimidation," and if burning a cross amounted to a true threat or act of intimidation, violators may be prosecuted. Justice O'Connor defined true threats as encompassing "those statements where the speaker means to communicate a serious expression of an intent to commit an act of unlawful violence to a particular individual or group of individuals."

On that point, Justice Scalia, in a separate opinion in part concurring and dissenting, and Justice Thomas, in a dissenting opinion, agreed with Justice O'Connor. However, Justice O'Connor also ruled that Virginia's law was unconstitutional because a section of the law dealing with jury instructions permitting the inference of intent to intimidate invited jurors to ignore "all of the contextual factors that are necessary to decide whether a particular cross burning [was] intended to intimidate," instead of expressing a political message. Justice Scalia disagreed with that part of Justice O'Connor's analysis and holding, contending that under the state statute a jury could be properly instructed and the inference of intimidation rebutted. In his dissent, Justice Thomas contended that the plurality went too far and that cross burning should never receive First Amendment protection because of its history and sole message of terror and intimidation.

Justice Souter, joined by Justices Kennedy and Ginsburg, filed a separate opinion in part concurring and dissenting. They agreed that Virginia's law was unconstitutional but maintained that the First Amendment forbids all content-based regulations of expression. Cross burning, in their view, was inherently symbolic and might convey not only a message of terror but also of political ideology. Accordingly, they would have held that no law punishing cross burning could survive First Amendment scrutiny.

Symbolic Expression and Speech-Plus-Conduct

Next to cross burning there is no more provocative or poignant political expression than the desecration of the American flag, precisely because of its political symbolism. The Court initially recognized the symbolism of flags and First Amendment protection for their use in expressive conduct in *Stromberg v. California* (1931).[18] There, Chief Justice Charles Evans Hughes struck down a state law prohibiting the display of a red flag as a symbol of opposition to the government, when overturning the conviction of a director of a Communist youth camp who raised the red flag every morning as part of the camp's daily activities. Then, in *West Virginia State Board of Education v. Barnette* (1943),[19] the Court struck down a state law *compelling* school children to salute the American flag at the start of each school day. In doing so, the Court reaffirmed that nonverbal expression receives First Amendment protection and that individuals may not be forced to participate in symbolic activities.

The Court underscored the principles announced in *Barnette* in *Wooley v. Maynard* (1977),[20] when striking down a New Hampshire law requiring passenger cars to carry license plates inscribed with the state's motto, "Live Free or Die." The Court found that the state's justification was not sufficiently compelling to override First Amendment interests. More specifically, Chief Justice Burger rejected the state's arguments that requiring the motto on passenger cars, but not on commercial vehicles, was an aid to police, and that the state had an interest in inculcating respect for history and authority.

The Court also found the protest of a group of black students standing silently in a "whites only" public library to be constitutionally protected symbolic expression.[21] But not all expressive symbolism and conduct receives First Amendment protection.[22] In *Clark v. Community for Creative Non-Violence* (1984),[23] for example, the Burger Court upheld that the National Park Service's regulations against camping in national parks not designated as campsites do not violate the First Amendment as applied to demonstrators who erected and slept in a tent city in Lafayette Park, Washington, D.C., as a way of dramatizing the plight of the needy and homeless. In reaffirming there that not all forms of symbolic speech-plus-conduct and nonverbal expression are protected, the Court applied a test created in *United States v. O'Brien* (1968).[24]

In *United States v. O'Brien*, the Warren Court held that burning draft cards at protest rallies against the Vietnam War was not protected symbolic speech. There, Chief Justice Warren set out certain guidelines for differentiating between protected and unprotected symbolic speech and conduct. Those guidelines are often referred to as the *O'Brien* four-prong test: (1) Is the regulation within Congress's authority to enact? (2) Does the regulation further a legitimate governmental interest? (3) Is the regulation unrelated to the suppression of speech per se? (4) Is the regulation only an incidental restriction on expression? Chief Justice Warren concluded that the ban on draft-card burning survived all of those concerns. Congress had the authority to ban draft-card burning because it has the power to raise an army, and the ban promoted the efficiency of the system. The chief justice also deemed the regulation to be unrelated to the suppression of speech per se, and to be only a minor incidental restriction, since antiwar protests could be expressed in other ways. He further explained:

We cannot accept the view that an apparently limitless variety of conduct can be labeled "speech" whenever the person engaging in the
conduct intends thereby to express an idea. . . . This Court has held
that when "speech" and "nonspeech" elements are combined in the
same course of conduct, a sufficiently important governmental interest in regulating the nonspeech element can justify incidental limitations on First Amendment freedoms. To characterize the quality of the
governmental interest which must appear, the Court has employed a
variety of descriptive terms: compelling, substantial, subordinating;
paramount, cogent, strong. Whatever imprecision inheres in these
terms, we think it clear that a government regulation is sufficiently
justified if it is within the constitutional power of Government; if it
furthers an important or substantial governmental interest; if the governmental interest is unrelated to the suppression of free expression;
and if the incidental restriction on alleged First Amendment freedoms
is no greater than is essential to the furtherance of that interest.

The American flag is one of the most potent national political
symbols. And the Court has often faced controversies over not just
the government's forcing individuals to participate in symbolic acts
honoring the flag, as in *Barnette* (discussed earlier), but over punishing individuals who use and abuse the flag as a means of expressing
their political views. The Court, for instance, upheld First Amendment protection for a protestor wearing a small American flag on
the seat of his pants,[25] and for a student who hung the American
flag upside down with a peace symbol attached on the window of a
dormitory room.[26]

The burning of the U.S. flag as a form of symbolic political protest
has also sharply divided the Court, no less than the country. In *Street
v. New York* (1969),[27] the Warren Court split five to four when overruling the conviction of a protestor who burned the flag after the
murder of civil rights activist James Meredith, in violation of a law
making it a misdemeanor to publicly mutilate, deface, or cast contempt on the flag "by words or act." There, Chief Justice Warren
and Justices Black, Fortas, and White dissented.

Twenty years later in another controversial five-to-four decision,
the Rehnquist Court once again upheld the First Amendment's protection for the symbolism of flag burning in *Texas v. Johnson*
(1989).[28] Gregory Johnson participated in political demonstrations

outside of the 1984 Republican National Convention in Dallas, Texas, to protest the policies of the Reagan administration. After a march through the streets, Johnson burned the American flag while protestors chanted "America, Red, White, and Blue. We Spit on You." No one was physically injured or threatened with injury. Johnson was arrested, tried, and convicted of flag desecration in violation of a Texas statute, and a state appeals court affirmed. However, the Texas Court of Criminal Appeals reversed, holding that Johnson's flag burning was expressive conduct protected by the First Amendment. That decision was affirmed by a bare majority of the Supreme Court. Writing for the majority, Justice Brennan applied the four-prong *O'Brien* test and sustained First Amendment protection for flag burning. Justices Stevens and Chief Justice Rehnquist, joined by Justices White and O'Connor, dissented.

In response to the Court's ruling in *Texas v. Johnson*, President George H. W. Bush and numerous members of Congress called for a constitutional amendment overturning that decision. Congress, though, instead passed the Federal Flag Protection Act of 1989, authorizing the prosecution of those who desecrate the American flag. That law was in turn immediately challenged and overturned by the same bare majority of the Court in *Texas v. Johnson*.[29] As in *Johnson*, the majority ruled that the federal statute "suffer[ed] from the same fundamental flaw" as the earlier state laws in aiming at "suppressing expression." Following that ruling, further attempts have been repeatedly made to pass a constitutional amendment granting Congress to enact a law forbidding desecration of the American flag, but have failed to win the required two-thirds approval of the Senate.[30]

Still, not all expressive conduct or *speech-plus-conduct* receives First Amendment protection.[31] Central to the Court's analysis of the permissibility of speech-plus-conduct—such as activities like peaceful picketing, boycotts, and demonstrations—is the concept of a *public forum*. The concept of public forums is based on the recognition of the importance of discussion of public affairs, however offensive, in public streets, parks, and facilities. The concept of a public forum was introduced into constitutional law by Justice Owen Roberts (1930–1945) in *Hague v. Committee for Industrial Organization (CIO)* (1939).[32] The CIO was denied permission to use public halls for a rally in Jersey City, New Jersey, and its members were arrested and removed from the city for publicly discussing and distributing leaflets on the labor movement. When striking down the city's ordinance prohibiting assemblies "in or upon public streets, highways, public parks or public buildings" without a permit from the director of public safety, Justice Roberts observed:

> Wherever the title of streets and parks may rest, they have immemorially been held in trust for the use of the public and, time out of mind, have been used for purposes of assembly, communicating thoughts between citizens, and discussing public questions. Such use of the streets and public places has, from ancient times, been a part of the privileges, immunities, rights and liberties of citizens. The privilege of a citizen of the United States to use the streets and parks for communication of views on national questions may not be regulated in the interest of all; it is not absolute, but relative, and must be exercised in consonance with peace and good order; but must not, in the guise of regulation, be abridged or denied.

The concept of a public forum has, on the one hand, been applied to the steps of state capitols,[33] and the streets surrounding state capitols,[34] streets and sidewalks near courthouses,[35] schools,[36] municipal auditoriums,[37] embassies,[38] criminal trials,[39] steps of the Supreme Court,[40] and central airport terminals.[41] The Court also held that, subject to certain restrictions, peaceful protests may be held in Lafayette Park, Washington, D.C.,[42] and that when state university facilities have been established as an open forum, they may not be denied use by religious groups or for religious expression.[43]

The Court has ruled, on the other hand, that nonpublic forums may be regulated and access conditioned or denied. Nonpublic forums limiting freedom of expression include bus placards[44] and the areas surrounding jails,[45] army bases,[46] military bases,[47] the property of U.S. post offices,[48] and airports.[49] The Court also held that televised debates may exclude "marginal" candidates and are not public forums,[50] that computers in public libraries that receive federal funding are not public forums,[51] and that localities may not be compelled to permit the erection of a monument in a public park because the decision to erect a monument is government-sponsored speech.[52]

When drawing the lines between public and nonpublic forums and constitutional protection for speech-plus-conduct, the Court has not taken a categorical approach. Instead, the Court has considered the circumstances and context in weighing claims to First Amendment freedoms and interests in safeguarding against harms to public safety and social order. In drawing those boundaries, the Court generally gives consideration to alternative venues for expression that is deemed offensive and provocative.

Student Expression and School Regulations

Student expression and school regulations is another special area where the Court has denied, but sometimes extended, First Amendment protection, even though it crosscuts rulings on symbolic speech, public forums, and other rulings on provocative and potentially disruptive expression, depending on the circumstances and context.

In general, students in colleges and universities have greater First Amendment protection than those in primary and secondary schools. The Court has held, for instance, that colleges and universities may not deny recognition to student organizations because of their political views,[53] or deny the expenditure of student activity funds for student groups engaged in religious expression,[54] or expel a college student for distributing allegedly indecent materials.[55] However, the Court has also ruled that even college student newspaper offices are not exempt from searches by police for photographs and other mere evidence of crime.[56]

While the First Amendment has been held to extend less protection to student expression in primary and secondary schools, the Court has ruled that students may not be compelled to salute the American flag at the start of the school day,[57] that schools may not *remove* books from libraries because they are deemed offensive to some students and parents,[58] and has upheld the Equal Access Act of 1984, which forbids public schools from discriminating against student meetings on school grounds on the basis of "religious, political, philosophical or other content of the speech at such meetings."[59] In addition, the Court has emphasized the importance of the free flow of ideas in schools: "The classroom is peculiarly the 'marketplace of ideas.' The Nation's future depends upon leaders trained through wide exposure to that robust exchange of ideas."[60]

Nonetheless, the Court has generally limited protection for student expression and approved broad discretion for school regulations. But it has done so on a case-by-case, highly contextualized, basis. Four rulings are illustrative of the Court's approaches to and standards for provocative and allegedly disruptive student expression: *Tinker v. Des Moines Independent Community School District* (1969),[61] *Bethel School District No. 403 v. Fraser* (1986),[62] *Hazelwood School District v. Kuhlmeier* (1988),[63] and *Morse v. Frederick* (2007).[64]

Tinker provides the classic example of First Amendment protection for student expression. In 1965 a group of adults and students in Des Moines, Iowa, decided to publicize their objections to the war in Vietnam by wearing black armbands during the Christmas season. The principals of the Des Moines public schools became aware of the plan and promptly adopted a policy forbidding the wearing of armbands in school and suspending any student who refused to comply. John Tinker, a fifteen-year-old high school student, and his sister Mary Beth, a thirteen-year-old, along with three others in the district of fifteen thousand students, wore black armbands to school and were suspended and sent home. They and their parents asked a federal district court for an injunction restraining school officials from enforcing the policy against wearing black armbands. The court, however, upheld the school's authority. On appeal, the Court of Appeals for the Eighth Circuit was evenly divided and accordingly upheld the lower court's ruling. The Tinkers, thereupon, appealed to the Supreme Court.

Writing for the Court in *Tinker*, Justice Fortas declared, "It can hardly be argued that either students or teachers shed their constitutional rights of freedom of speech or expression at the schoolhouse gate," and characterized the armbands as virtually "pure speech" entitled to "comprehensive protection under the First Amendment." When provocative student expression collides with school regulations—whether in the classroom, cafeteria, or on the playing field—Justice Fortas ruled that students "may express [their] opinions, even on controversial subjects like the conflict in Vietnam, if [they do] so without 'materially and substantially interfer[ing] with the requirements of appropriate discipline in the operation of the school' and without colliding with the rights of others." By contrast, dissenting Justices Black and Harlan disagreed. Justice Black, the "First Amendment absolutist," countered that, although the students had not made offensive or boisterous remarks, the armbands were disruptive and took other students' minds off their class work.

Almost twenty years later, the Burger Court went the other way in limiting First Amendment protection for student expression in _Bethel School District No. 403 v. Fraser._ Matthew N. Fraser, a student at Bethel School, delivered at a school assembly a speech nominating a fellow student for student elective office. Approximately six hundred high school students attended and were required to do so, or to report to study hall. The assembly was part of a school-sponsored educational program in self-government. During the entire speech, Fraser referred to his candidate in terms of a graphic and explicit sexual metaphor, but not obscene language. Two of Fraser's teachers, with whom he discussed the contents of the speech in advance, informed him that the speech was "inappropriate and that he probably should not deliver it," as well as that his delivery of the speech might have "severe consequences." A Bethel disciplinary rule provided that "[c]onduct which materially and substantially interferes with the educational process is prohibited, including the use of obscene, profane language or gestures." The morning after the assembly, the assistant principal called Fraser into her office and notified him that the school considered his speech to have been a violation of that rule.

Writing for the Court, Chief Justice Burger did not quote Fraser's speech but emphasized that "it is a highly appropriate function of public school education to prohibit the use of vulgar and offensive terms in public discourse. A high school assembly or classroom is no place for a sexually explicit monologue directed towards an unsuspecting audience of teenage students." Moreover, Chief Justice Burger distinguished between _Tinker's_ political message of wearing armbands as a symbolic protest and the sexual content of Fraser's speech. "The undoubted freedom to advocate unpopular and controversial views in schools and classrooms," continued Chief Justice Burger, "must be balanced against the society's countervailing interest in teaching students the boundaries of socially appropriate behavior." On that basis the chief justice set forth another standard for student expression, observing that because school officials have an "interest in teaching students the boundaries of socially appropriate behavior, they can censor student speech that is vulgar or indecent, even if it does not cause a 'material or substantial disruption.'"

Concurring in *Bethel*, Justice Brennan, who usually championed First Amendment freedoms, quoted Fraser's speech in full:

> "I know a man who is firm—he's firm in his pants, he's firm in his shirt, his character is firm—but most . . . of all, his belief in you, the students of Bethel, is firm. Jeff Kuhlman is a man who takes his point and pounds it in. If necessary. He'll take an issue and nail it to the wall. He doesn't attack in spurts—he drives hard, pushing and pushing until finally—he succeeds. Jeff is a man who will go to the very end—even the climax, for each and every one of you. So vote for Jeff for A.S.B. vice-president—he'll never come between you and the best our high school can be."

He did so in order to dispute Chief Justice Burger's characterization of the speech as "obscene," "vulgar," "lewd," and "offensively lewd." Still, like Justice Black in *Tinker*, Justice Brennan concluded that Fraser's speech was disruptive and that school authorities had the power to "prevent disruption of school educational activities."

Justices Marshall and Stevens dissented in *Bethel*, the latter explaining:

> "Frankly, my dear, I don't give a damn."
>
> When I was in a high school student, the use of those words in public forums shocked the Nation. Today Clark Gable's four-letter expletive is less offensive than it was then. Nevertheless, I assume that high school administrators may prohibit the use of that word in classroom discussion and even in extracurricular activities that are sponsored by the school and held on school premises. For I believe a school faculty must regulate the content as well as the style of student speech

in carrying out its educational mission. It does seem to me, however, that if a student is to be punished for using offensive speech, he is entitled to fair notice of the scope of the prohibition and the consequence of its violation. The interest in free speech protected by the First Amendment and the interest in fair procedure protected by the Due Process Clause of the Fourteenth Amendment combine to require this conclusion.

The Court further limited student expression in *Kuhlmeier*. At issue was a school's censorship of articles on birth control and divorce in a student newspaper. Writing for the majority, with Justices Brennan, Marshall, and Blackmun dissenting, Justice White distinguished *Tinker* on the ground that student newspapers are school-sponsored activities, and thus schools are neither passive observers nor public forums:

> School facilities may be deemed to be public forums only if school authorities have "by policy or by practice" opened those facilities "for indiscriminate use by the general public," or by some segment of the public, such as student organizations. If the facilities have instead been reserved for other intended purposes, then no public forum has been created, and school officials may impose reasonable restrictions on the speech of students, teachers, and other members of the school community.

Accordingly, Justice White laid out another standard for schools' regulation of student speech: "[E]ducators do not offend the First Amendment by exercising editorial control over the style and content of student speech in school-sponsored expressive activities so long as their actions are reasonably related to legitimate pedagogical concerns."

Finally, in *Morse v. Frederick*, the Roberts Court upheld further restrictions on student expression with a new twist and test. Juneau-Douglas High School in Juneau, Alaska, released its students to observe the Winter Olympics Torch Relay, sponsored by Coca-Cola and other private sponsors. Joseph Frederick and some other students stood on the sidewalk across from the school to observe the event. When television cameras could view it, they unfurled a banner that read "Bong Hits 4 Jesus." Deborah Morse, the school principal, promptly crossed over the street, grabbed, and crumpled the banner. Subsequently, she suspended Frederick for ten days for violating the school's policy against displaying offensive material and promoting the use of illegal drugs. Frederick countered that the display was humorous and meaningless. After appealing to the local school board, he filed a lawsuit in federal district court, contending that his First Amendment rights were violated and asking that the suspension be removed from his high school records.

A federal district court rejected Frederick's claims, reasoning that *Bethel*, not *Tinker*, applied and that students' freedom of expression may be suppressed if officials reasonably "forecast substantial disruptions of or material interference with school activities." On appeal, the Court of Appeals for the Ninth Circuit reversed, reasoning that the precedent in *Bethel* embraced only offensive speech that was "sexual in nature" and the circumstances here were different from those in *Kuhlmeier*. As a result, *Tinker* was controlling and Frederick couldn't be punished for speech that did not disrupt the school's functioning. Morse appealed that decision, and the Supreme Court reversed the appellate court's decision.

Writing for the majority in *Morse v. Frederick*, Chief Justice Roberts observed that the issue was "whether a principal may, consistent with the First Amendment, restrict student speech at a school event, when that speech is reasonably viewed as promoting illegal drug use." Although the message was deemed "gibberish," Chief Justice Roberts observed that Morse "had to decide to act—or not act—on the spot. . . . Failing to act would send a powerful message to the students in her charge, including Frederick, about how serious the school was about the dangers of illegal drug use." Chief Justice Roberts distinguished *Morse* from *Kuhlmeier* and *Bethel*: "*Kuhlmeier* does not control this case," he observed, "because no one would reasonably believe that Frederick's banner bore the school's imprimatur," while adding that *Bethel* "should not be read to encompass any speech that could fit under some definition of 'offensive.' After all, much political and religious speech might be perceived as offensive to some." Nonetheless, Chief Justice Roberts ruled that school authorities may restrict student expression that promotes illegal drug use, even if that expression occurs off campus and on a public street near the school.

Joining the Court's opinion in *Morse v. Frederick*, in a concurring opinion Justices Samuel Alito (2006–) and Kennedy emphasized the narrowness of the decision as limited to student expression interpreted to advocate illegal drug use, while concurring Justice Thomas deemed *Tinker* as having no basis in the First Amendment and ought to be overruled. Justice Stevens, joined by Justices Souter and Ginsburg, dissented, observing that

> the First Amendment protects student speech if the message itself neither violates a permissible rule nor expressly advocates conduct that is illegal and harmful to students. This nonsense banner does neither, and the Court does serious violence to the First Amendment in upholding—indeed, lauding—a school's decision to punish Frederick for expressing a view with which it disagreed.

For his part, Justice Breyer issued a separate opinion, in part concurring and dissenting, countering that the majority's opinion provided little guidance for schools and lower courts.

As a result of the Court's rulings in *Tinker*, *Bethel*, *Kuhlmeier*, and *Morse*, schools' regulations of student expression are wide ranging, but increasingly suppressive, and state and lower federal courts' rulings conflict.[65] The Court's standards are also rather confusing—whereas *Tinker* upheld First Amendment protection for students' symbolic political expression, *Bethel* upheld content-based restrictions for student speech that is allegedly lewd or obscene, and *Morse* upheld school policies applied to expression deemed to advocate drug usage. Moreover, the Court is likely to confront in the near future other regulations of student expression in "cyberspeech" via e-mails and networking sites such as Facebook, MySpace, and Twitter, as well as whether that expression is uploaded from computers on or off school grounds.

Conclusion

In sum, the Supreme Court has rendered the category of "fighting words" virtually null and extended First Amendment protection to politically symbolic expression and public forums. The Court, however, has declined to extend that protection to other forms of expression, such as true threats, nonpublic forums, and student expression in a number of cases. Notably, it has not done so based on a categorical or definitional approach, but rather on a case-by-case basis, depending on the contexts and circumstances of provocative and potentially disruptive expression.

6

Conclusion

THE FIRST AMENDMENT is not an absolute, nor could (or should) it be. Congress regulates large areas of expression and communication—such as false and deceptive advertising, fraud, insider trading, copyright, trademarks, and perjury, among other areas (as discussed in chapter 1). Outside of such areas the Supreme Court in the twentieth century expanded First Amendment protection for a broad range of expression, except for four categories of constitutionally unprotected expression—obscenity, defamation, commercial speech, and "fighting words."

Yet the Court's categorical or definitional approach to such unprotected expression provides at best a baseline framework for analysis. The category of obscenity, for example, now applies principally to only hard-core and child pornography. And the category of "fighting words" has been rendered virtually null, while the Court has incrementally expanded First Amendment protection for commercial speech.

Beyond those categories of unprotected speech, the Court at the same time has nonetheless recognized other content-based restrictions on expression based on their context and circumstances. The Court has (as previously discussed) upheld restrictions on true threats and provocative and allegedly indecent expression on broadcast radio and television, for example, along with that of students' expression in a range of circumstances.

As technology advances and new First Amendment challenges arise, the Court may well find new categories of constitutionally unprotected expression or further content-based exceptions to its categorical approach to freedom of expression, such as regulations prohibiting the sale of violent videos to minors.

In its 2009–2010 term, for instance, the Court confronted a challenge to Congress's enactment of the Depiction of Animal Cruelty Act of 1999.[1] That law authorized a fine and imprisonment for up to five years, or both, for anyone who depicted for commercial gain a sound, electronic, or video recording of "conduct in which a living animal is intentionally maimed, mutilated, tortured, wounded, or killed." Congress, in response to animal rights and other interest groups, aimed to criminalize so-called crush videos—videos that show small animals being crushed or stamped to death. An exception was made for depictions that have "serious religious, political, scientific, educational, journalistic, historical, or artistic value."

Robert J. Stevens was convicted under the statute for selling videos of dog fights and sentenced to thirty-seven months in prison. The U.S. Court of Appeals for the Third Circuit, however, reversed the lower court's decision and held that the law did not fit within any of the four categories of constitutionally unprotected expression.[2] In doing so, it rejected the position of Republican President George W. Bush's administration that the statute was constitutionally permissible under the First Amendment, and ruled instead that it was "an unconstitutional infringement on free speech rights guaranteed by the First Amendment." In an appeal of the Third Circuit's decision in *United States v. Stevens*, Democratic President Barack Obama's solicitor general, Elena Kagan, continued to press the view that, although "the depictions at issue here do not fall into any established category of unprotected speech," the statute should be upheld as within Congress's power and the appellate court's decision reversed, "because of the many harms [fighting dogs] cause: injury to the dogs themselves, injury to humans attacked by vicious dogs, increased gambling and other criminal activity, and debilitating effects on public mores."[3] The government in effect asked the Court to recognize a new category of constitutionally unprotected expression or another content-based restriction. In other words, the government

urged the Court to expand the categories of unprotected speech recognized in *Chaplinsky* and later rulings, or alternatively uphold restrictions on depictions of animal cruelty as it did with respect to
child pornography in *New York v. Ferber* (1982).[4]

In a rather sweeping opinion for the Court in *United States v. Stevens* (2010),[5] Chief Justice John Roberts Jr. affirmed the appellate
court's decision and struck down the federal statute. In doing so, the
chief justice emphasized the historically narrow categories of constitutionally unprotected expression. In his words, and quoting from
earlier decisions:

> The First Amendment provides that "Congress shall make no law . . .
> abridging the freedom of speech." "[A]s a general matter, the First
> Amendment means that government has no power to restrict expres-
> sion because of its message, its ideas, its subject matter, or its
> content. . . .
>
> "From 1791 to the present," however, the First Amendment has
> "permitted restrictions upon the content of speech in a few limited
> areas," and has never "include[d] a freedom to disregard these tradi-
> tional limitations." These "historic and traditional categories long
> familiar to the bar"—including obscenity, defamation, fraud, incite-
> ment, and speech integral to criminal conduct—are "well-defined and
> narrowly limited classes of speech, the prevention and punishment of
> which have never been thought to raise any Constitutional problem."

Chief Justice Roberts proceeded to reject the government's arguments for carving out a separate category of unprotected expression
for depictions of animal cruelty, based on a social costs-and-benefits
analysis. More specifically, Chief Justice Roberts rejected the analogy
drawn by the government between an exception for child pornography, upheld in *New York v. Ferber*, and depictions of animal cruelty,
explaining that

> [w]hen we have identified categories of speech as fully outside the
> protection of the First Amendment, it has not been on the basis of a
> simple cost-benefit analysis. In *Ferber*, for example, we classified child
> pornography as such a category. We noted that the State of New York
> had a compelling interest in protecting children from abuse, and that
> the value of using children in these works (as opposed to simulated

conduct or adult actors) was *de minimis*. But our decision did not rest on this "balance of competing interests" alone. We made clear that *Ferber* presented a special case: The market for child pornography was "intrinsically related" to the underlying abuse, and was therefore "an integral part of the production of such materials, an activity illegal throughout the Nation." As we noted, "[i]t rarely has been suggested that the constitutional freedom for speech and press extends its immunity to speech or writing used as an integral part of conduct in violation of a valid criminal statute." *Ferber* thus grounded its analysis in a previously recognized, long-established category of unprotected speech, and our subsequent decisions have shared this understanding.

Our decisions in *Ferber* and other cases cannot be taken as establishing a freewheeling authority to declare new categories of speech outside the scope of the First Amendment. Maybe there are some categories of speech that have been historically unprotected, but have not yet been specifically identified or discussed as such in our case law. But if so, there is no evidence that "depictions of animal cruelty" is among them. We need not foreclose the future recognition of such additional categories to reject the Government's highly manipulable balancing test as a means of identifying them.

Only Justice Samuel Alito dissented from the Court's ruling in *United States v. Stevens*, observing that

> [t]he Court strikes down in its entirety a valuable statute that was enacted not to suppress speech, but to prevent horrific acts of animal cruelty—in particular, the creation and commercial exploitation of "crush videos," a form of depraved entertainment that has no social value. The Court's approach, which has the practical effect of legalizing the sale of such videos and is thus likely to spur a resumption of their production, is unwarranted.

In sum, a solid majority in *United States v. Stevens* underscored its reluctance to expand the categories of First Amendment unprotected expression. Nonetheless, as in the past and no doubt in future cases, the Court will continue to confront the fundamental questions (stated at the outset): Why do we, as citizens no less than Congress and the Court, value freedom of expression? Is it because freedom of expression has an *instrumental* value in promoting democracy and self-governance? Is it because freedom of expression has *intrinsic value* and is essential to individual self-expression and self-determination? Is it because, as Justice Holmes argued, the best test of truth is determined by "the marketplace of ideas"? Or is it because once expression is regulated, censored, and punished, the proverbial "slippery slope" of governmental censorship becomes wide open? Or, perhaps, is it because of all the above rationales, depending on the contexts, under what circumstances, and how harms—public and private—are weighed against First Amendment guarantees for freedom of expression?

Appendix

Unprotected Speech Time Line

Laura Brookover

1791	Text of the First Amendment is by its express terms limited to "Congress" and does not refer to the other branches of the federal government or to the states. All the provisions in the Bill of Rights—including the First Amendment—officially are ratified on December 15.
1798	The Federalist-dominated Congress passes a series of laws known as the Alien and Sedition Acts. The Sedition Act makes it a crime to publish "false, scandalous, or malicious writing" against the government. Officials use the law as a means to target Democratic-Republican newspaper editors.
1801	The Sedition Act expires under the presidency of Thomas Jefferson, a Democratic-Republican who despised the law.
1821	In *Commonwealth v. Sharpless*, 2 Serg & R. 91 (Pa. 1815), the Pennsylvania high court rules that an obscene painting in a private home could give rise to criminal sanctions.

1836 The U.S. House of Representatives adopts gag rules preventing discussion of antislavery proposals. (The House repeals the rules in 1844.)

1842 The Tariff Act is amended to authorize customs officers to seize imported prints and pictures that are "obscene or immoral" and thereafter to go to court to request their destruction.

1863 General Ambrose Burnside of the Union Army orders the suspension of the publication of the *Chicago Times* on account of repeated expression of disloyal and incendiary sentiments. President Lincoln rescinds Burnside's order three days later.

1864 By order of President Lincoln, General John A. Dix, a Union commander, suppresses the *New York Journal of Commerce* and the *New York World* and arrests the newspapers' editors after both papers publish a forged presidential proclamation purporting to order another draft of four hundred thousand men. Lincoln withdraws the order to arrest the editors and the papers resume publication two days later.

1865 Congress enacts a law to prohibit the distribution of obscene books and pictures in the U.S. mail.

1873 The Comstock Act makes it a crime to send "obscene, lewd, and/or lascivious" materials or information relating to contraceptives or abortion through the mail.

1907 *Patterson v. Colorado.* Leaving undecided the question of whether First Amendment guarantees are applicable to the states via the Fourteenth Amendment, the Court holds that the free speech and press guarantees only guard against prior restraint and do not prevent "subsequent punishment."

1915 *Mutual Film Corp. v. Industrial Commission of Ohio.* The Supreme Court upholds an Ohio statute restricting the content of films shown in Ohio, holding that free speech protection did not extend to motion pictures. (Later overruled by *Joseph Burstyn, Inc. v. Wilson* in 1952.)

1917   Congress passes the Espionage Act, which imposes heavy penalties for anyone causing or attempting to cause "insubordination, disloyalty, mutiny, or refusal of duty" in the U.S. military.

1918   Congress passes the Sedition Act, which prohibits Americans from using "disloyal, profane, scurrilous, or abusive language" about the U.S. government, flag, or military. (Congress repeals the Sedition Act in 1920.)

1919–1921   The Justice and Immigration Departments conduct raids, known as "Palmer raids" after the then attorney general, on suspected radical leftists.

1919   *Schenck v. United States.* The Supreme Court upholds a conviction under the Espionage Act, and Oliver Wendell Holmes Jr. sets forth the "clear and present danger" test.

1926   H. L. Mencken is arrested for distributing copies of *American Mercury.* Censorship groups in Boston contend the periodical is obscene.

1925–1927   *Gitlow v. New York* and *Fiske v. Kansas.* The Supreme Court recognizes that the First Amendment guarantee for freedom of speech applies to the states, as well as a limitation on Congress.

1931   *Near v. Minnesota.* The Supreme Court strikes down a Minnesota nuisance law that allowed officials to close down newspapers that printed articles they found offensive. The Court expresses reservations about laws that constitute a prior restraint on expression and applies the First Amendment guarantee for freedom of the press to the states.

1938   *Life* magazine is banned in the United States for publishing pictures from the public health film, *The Birth of a Baby.*

1940   The Smith Act (Title I of the Alien Registration Act of 1940) makes punishable the advocacy of the "propriety of overthrowing the Government of the United States or of any State by force or violence" and is used to prosecute many Communist Party leaders. The statute remains on the books.

1941   Congress authorizes President Franklin D. Roosevelt to create the Office of Censorship.

1942   *Chaplinsky v. New Hampshire.* The Supreme Court rules that "fighting words" are not constitutionally protected, nor are those words "which by their very utterance inflict injury or tend to incite an immediate breach of the peace."

1942   *Valentine v. Chrestensen.* The Supreme Court rules that purely commercial advertising receives no First Amendment protection.

1943   *National Broadcasting Co. v. United States.* The Supreme Court rules that no one has a First Amendment right to a radio license or to monopolize a radio frequency.

1945   *Associated Press v. United States.* The Supreme Court holds that the application of the Sherman Act to a group of publishers found in violation of the antitrust law did not violate the First Amendment's protection of a free press, noting that "freedom to combine to keep others from publishing is not" a protected right.

1949   *Kovacs v. Cooper.* The Supreme Court upholds a local ordinance banning the use of sound systems that emit "loud and raucous" noises on public streets.

1951   *Dennis v. United States.* The Supreme Court upholds a conviction under the Smith Act through a narrow and reworked application of the clear and present danger test, asking "whether the gravity of the evil, discounted by its improbability, justifies such invasion of free speech as is necessary to avoid the danger."

1951   *Feiner v. New York.* The Supreme Court upholds a disorderly conduct conviction for a young protestor based on the hostile reaction of a nearby crowd of people.

1957   *Roth v. United States.* The Supreme Court holds that obscenity is not protected under the Constitution, defining obscenity as material appealing to the "prurient interest" according to "contemporary community standards."

1959   *Barenblatt v. United States.* The Supreme Court upholds the conviction of a college professor who, during testimony before the House Committee on Un-American Activities, refused on First Amendment grounds to say whether he had ever been a member of the Communist Party.

1964   *New York Times Co. v. Sullivan.* The Supreme Court rules that public officials cannot recover damages for libel unless they show by clear and convincing evidence that the speaker (in this case a newspaper) acted with actual malice, defined as acting with knowing falsity or reckless disregard for the truth or falsity of a statement.

1968   Congress passes a national flag-desecration law that imposes criminal penalties on anyone who "knowingly casts contempt upon any flag of the United States by publicly mutilating, defacing, defiling, burning, or trampling upon it."

1968   *United States v. O'Brien.* The Supreme Court upholds a criminal prohibition against burning draft cards. The Court establishes a test for evaluating restrictions on communication that contains both speech and nonspeech elements.

1968   *Pickering v. Board of Education*. The Supreme Court rules that a public school teacher has a First Amendment right to speak as a citizen on a matter of public concern.

1969   *Watts v. United States*. The Supreme Court explains that true threats are not protected speech but rules that a young war protestor did not utter such a true threat at a demonstration in Washington, D.C.

1969   *Brandenburg v. Ohio*. The Supreme Court reverses the conviction of a Ku Klux Klan leader for a speech he made at a Klan rally, but nonetheless states that speech advocating the use of force or crime is not protected if it is directed at producing "imminent" action and is "likely" to cause such action.

1969   *Red Lion Broadcasting Co. v. Federal Communications Commission*. The Supreme Court finds that Congress and the FCC did not violate the First Amendment when they required a radio or television station to allow response time to persons subjected to personal attacks and political editorializing on air.

1970   *Rowan v. United States Post Office*. The Supreme Court upholds the constitutionality of a statute that permits the postal service at an individual's request to order that a sender remove the individual from its mailing list.

1972   *Lloyd Corp. v. Tanner*. The Supreme Court holds that there is no First Amendment right to free expression on private property.

1973   *Miller v. California*. The Supreme Court affirms its ruling in *Roth* that obscenity is not protected by the First Amendment and establishes a three-prong test for determining what constitutes obscenity.

1973   *Paris Adult Theatre I v. Slaton*. The Supreme Court upholds a state law regulating obscene materials displayed at an "adult" theater, even where access to those materials is limited to adults.

1976   *Young v. American Mini Theatres*. The Supreme Court upholds the constitutionality of a local zoning ordinance that distinguished between movie theaters exhibiting sexually explicit "adult" films and those that did not.

1976   *Virginia State Board of Pharmacy v. Virginia Citizens Consumer Council*. The Supreme Court rules that truthful commercial speech is entitled to some First Amendment protection in a case involving pharmacy price advertising.

1977   *Bates v. State Bar of Arizona*. The Supreme Court rules that truthful attorney advertising is a form of commercial speech deserving of First Amendment protection.

1978   *Federal Communications Commission v. Pacifica*. The Supreme Court upholds the FCC's regulation of offensive words dealing with sex and excretion in radio broadcasts.

1981   *Heffron v. International Society for Krishna Consciousness*. The Supreme Court upholds a state requirement that religious organizations that wish to sell and distribute religious information be confined to an assigned location at the state fair.

1982   *New York v. Ferber*. The Supreme Court rules that child pornography is not protected by the First Amendment.

1985   *Harper & Row Publishers v. Nation Enterprises*. The Supreme Court holds that there is no First Amendment right to publish copyrighted material regarding public figures that would exceed the boundaries of "fair use."

1986   *City of Renton v. Playtime Theaters.* The Supreme Court upholds the constitutionality of a zoning ordinance that prohibits adult film theaters from standing within one thousand feet of any residential zone, single- or multi-family dwelling, church, park, or school.

1986   *Bethel School District v. Fraser.* The Supreme Court upholds a high school's disciplinary action against a student who gave a speech containing sexual innuendos at a school assembly.

1987   *Turner v. Safley.* The Supreme Court upholds a regulation restricting prison inmates' ability to correspond with other inmates through mail, stating that it was reasonably related to legitimate security concerns.

1988   *Hazelwood School District v. Kuhlmeier.* The Supreme Court rules that schools may regulate the contents of school-sponsored student publications if such regulation is "reasonably related to a legitimate pedagogical" purpose.

1989   *Texas v. Johnson.* The Supreme Court strikes down a Texas flag-desecration law on First Amendment grounds.

1989   Congress passes the Flag Protection Act. The act punishes anyone who "knowingly mutilates, defaces, physically defiles, burns, maintains on the floor or ground, or tramples upon any U.S. flag." (Ruled unconstitutional later in 1990 in *United States v. Eichman.*)

1990   A flag-desecration constitutional amendment is introduced in the U.S. Congress. It provides that "the Congress and the States have the power to prohibit the physical desecration of the flag of the United States." Measure fails.

1991   *Rust v. Sullivan.* The Supreme Court upholds the Department of Health and Human Services' requirement that family planning centers receiving federal funding must not discuss abortion as a method of family planning.

1994   *Madsen v. Women's Health Center.* The Supreme Court upholds a state court injunction limiting the locations outside of an abortion clinic in which antiabortion protestors may demonstrate.

1995   After the House votes 312 to 120 for a flag-desecration amendment, the measure fails in the Senate by three votes.

1997   *Schenck v. Pro-Choice Network of Western New York.* The Supreme Court upholds the validity of a fixed buffer zone outside of an abortion clinic into which antiabortion protestors may not enter, but strikes down a floating buffer zone that surrounds vehicles and patients entering or leaving the clinic.

1997   *Reno v. ACLU.* The Supreme Court strikes down portions of the Communications Decency Act, which criminalized the online transmission of patently offensive and indecent speech.

1998   The Child Online Protection Act (COPA), which attaches federal criminal liability to the online transmission for commercial purposes of material considered harmful to minors, is enacted by Congress.

1998   *National Endowment for the Arts v. Finley.* The Supreme Court upholds a statute requiring the NEA to take into consideration general standards of "decency and respect" for beliefs and values of the American public in its review of grant applications.

2000   *Hill v. Colorado.* The Supreme Court upholds a Colorado statute establishing a one-hundred-square-foot buffer zone outside of hospitals within which a person may not approach another person "within 8 feet" for the purpose of passing out literature or engaging in "oral protest, education, or counseling."

2000   *City of Erie v. Pap's A. M.* The Supreme Court upholds a city ordinance prohibiting public nudity and requiring the use of G-strings and pasties in nude dancing as a "content-neutral restriction that regulates conduct" under the framework set forth in *O'Brien*.

2002   *City of Los Angeles v. Alameda Books.* The Supreme Court upholds a local zoning ordinance limiting the number of adult entertainment business at a single location although the city did not study the negative effects of multiple such businesses in one location, because the city appropriately concluded in line with *Renton* that such an ordinance would "promote the city's interest in reducing crime."

2002   *Ashcroft v. Free Speech Coalition.* The Supreme Court strikes down two provisions of the Child Pornography Prevention Act designed to address the problem of virtual child porn.

2003   *United States v. American Libraries Association.* The Supreme Court upholds the Children's Internet Protection Act, a federal law that requires public libraries and public schools to install filtering software on computers to receive federal funding.

2003   *Eldred v. Ashcroft.* The Supreme Court holds that Congress is not constrained by the First Amendment from extending for a period of years the duration of copyrights.

2003   *Virginia v. Black.* The Supreme Court upholds a state law banning the burning of crosses if such conduct amounts to a "true threat." The Court strikes down a provision of the law that created a presumption that all cross burnings were done with the intent to intimidate.

2003   *McConnell v. Federal Election Commission.* The Supreme Court upholds the constitutionality of most of the Bipartisan Campaign Reform Act of 2002, which regulates the financing of political campaigns.

2004   *Ashcroft v. ACLU.* The Supreme Court affirms the rulings of lower federal courts that determine that the federal law known as the Child Online Protection Act violates the First Amendment.

2006   *Garcetti v. Ceballos.* The Supreme Court rules that public employees have no First Amendment protection for speech made pursuant to their official job duties.

2007   *Morse v. Frederick.* The Supreme Court establishes that "drug speech" in schools may be regulated as an exception to the Court's seminal student speech ruling in *Tinker v. Des Moines Independent Community School District.*

2008   *United States v. Williams.* The Supreme Court upholds the so-called PROTECT Act (Prosecutorial Remedies and Other Tools to end the Exploitation of Children Today Act of 2003), enacted after the Court's ruling in *Ashcroft v. Free Speech Coalition*, which makes it a federal crime to pander child pornography on the Internet.

2009   *Federal Communications Commission v. Fox Television Stations.* Upheld the extension of the FCC's ban on indecent communications, upheld in *Federal Communications Commission v. Pacifica Foundation*, to fleeting images and language on broadcast television.

**Laura Brookover is a second-year student at Georgetown University Law Center.

Notes

Foreword

1. See *Virginia v. West Virginia*, 78 U.S. 39 (1870).

2. In earlier drafts Madison was similarly categorical: "The people shall not be deprived or abridged of their right to speak, to write, or to publish their sentiments; and the freedom of the press, as one of the great bulwarks of liberty, shall be inviolable." Neil H. Cogan, ed., *The Complete Bill of Rights: The Drafts, Debates, Sources, and Origins* (New York: Oxford University Press, 1997), 83.

3. Edmund Cahn, "Justice Black and First Amendment 'Absolutes': A Public Interview," 37 *New York University Law Review* 549, 553 (1962).

4. See, for example, Black's vote in *Valentine v. Chrestensen*, 316 U.S. 52 (1942) (no protection for commercial speech), and his opinion in *Tinker v. Des Moines Independent Community School Dist.*, 393 U.S. 503 (1969) (student symbolic expression not protected under First Amendment).

5. *Chaplinsky v. New Hampshire*, 315 U.S. 568, 571–572 (1942). Justice Black joined in this opinion.

6. See, for example, *New York Times Co. v. Sullivan*, 376 U.S. 254 (1964) (libel); *Cohen v. California*, 403 U.S. 15 (1971) (profanity); *R. A. V. v. City of St. Paul*, 505 U.S. 377 (1992) (regarding fighting words, contrast Justice Scalia's majority opinion, extending protection to some kinds of fighting words, with Justice White's separate opinion objecting to any protection for fighting words).

7. *United States v. Stevens*, merits brief, June 2009, docket No. 08-769, 10–34.

8. C. Herman Pritchett, *Liberties and the Vinson Court* (Chicago: University of Chicago Press, 1954), 239. David O'Brien, like the author of this foreword, studied with Professor Pritchett during his tenure at the University of California at Santa Barbara.

9. *Terminiello v. Chicago*, 337 U.S. 1, 37 (1949) (J. Jackson, dissenting: "There is danger that, if the Court does not temper its doctrinaire logic with a little practical wisdom, it will convert the constitutional Bill of Rights into a suicide pact.")

10. See, for example, Pierre Schlag and David Skover, *Tactics of Legal Reasoning* (Durham, N.C.: Carolina Academic Press, 1986), 41–42.

Chapter 1

1. James Morton Smith, *Freedom's Fetters: The Alien and Sedition Laws and American Civil Liberties* (Ithaca, N.Y.: Cornell University Press, 1956), 185; David Cole, *Enemy Aliens: Double Standards and Constitutional Freedoms in the War on Terrorism* (New York: The New Press, 2003); and Geoffrey R. Stone, *Perilous Times: Free Speech in Wartime from the Espionage Act of 1798 to the War on Terrorism* (New York: W. W. Norton, 2004).

2. *New York Times Company v. Sullivan*, 376 U.S. 254 (1964). For further discussion, see chapter 3 and Anthony Lewis, *Make No Law: The Sullivan Case and the First Amendment* (New York: Random House, 1991), 144–45.

3. Sir William Blackstone, *Commentaries on the Laws of England* (Clarendon Press, 1766), 4:151–52. For further discussion of the common-law view and the framers' views of freedom of expression, see David M. O'Brien, *Constitutional Law and Politics*, vol. 2, *Civil Rights and Civil Liberties*, seventh edition (New York: W. W. Norton, 2007).

4. *Robertson v. Baldwin*, 165 U.S. 275, 281 (1897). See also *Prudential Insurance Company v. Cheek*, 259 U.S. 530 (1922).

5. *Patterson v. Colorado*, 205 U.S. 454, 462 (1907).

6. See *Near v. Minnesota*, 283 U.S. 697 (1931); *Gitlow v. New York*, 268 U.S. 652 (1925); and *Gilbert v. Minnesota*, 254 U.S. 325 (1920).

7. *Gitlow v. New York*, 268 U.S. 652 (1925).

8. *Schenck v. United States*, 249 U.S. 47 (1919).

9. See also *Pierce v. United States*, 252 U.S. 239 (1920).

10. *Debs v. United States*, 249 U.S. 211 (1919); and *Frowerk v. United States*, 249 U.S. 204 (1919).

11. *Abrams v. United States*, 250 U.S. 616 (1919). See also Richard Polenberg, *Fighting Faiths: The Abrams Case, the Supreme Court, and Free Speech* (New York: Viking Press, 1987).

12. See *Schaefer v. United States*, 251 U.S. 466 (1920); *Pierce v. United States*, 252 U.S. 239 (1920); *Gilbert v. Minnesota*, 254 U.S. 235 (1920); *Gitlow v. New York*, 268 U.S. 652 (1925); and *Whitney v. California*, 274 U.S. 357 (1927).

13. *Gitlow v. New York*, 268 U.S. 652 (1925).

14. *Whitney v. California*, 274 U.S. 357 (1927).

15. *Near v. Minnesota*, 283 U.S. 697 (1931). For further discussion, see Fred Friendly, *Minnesota Rag: The Dramatic Story of the Landmark Supreme Court Case That Gave New Meaning to Freedom of the Press* (New York: Random House, 1981).

16. *Near v. Minnesota*, 283 U.S. 697, 717 (1931).

17. *Grosjean v. American Press Co.*, 297 U.S. 233, 248–249 (1936).

18. *Cantwell v. Connecticut*, 310 U.S. 296 (1940).

19. See *Cantwell v. Connecticut*, 310 U.S. 296 (1940); *Douglas v. City of Jeanette*, 319 U.S. 157 (1943); *Jones v. Opelika*, 319 U.S. 102 (1943); *Murdock v. Pennsylvania*, 319 U.S. 105 (1943); and *Follet v. Town of McCormick*, 321 U.S. 573 (1944).

20. See *Joseph Burstyn, Inc. v. Wilson*, 343 U.S. 495 (1952), overruling *Mutual Film Corporation v. Industrial Commission of Ohio*, 236 U.S. 230 (1915). See also *Jacobellis v. Ohio*, 378 U.S. 184 (1964); *Freedman v. Maryland*, 380 U.S. 51 (1965); *United States v. 12 200-Ft. Reels of Super 8-mm. Film*, 413 U.S. 123 (1973); *Jenkins v. Georgia*, 418 U.S. 153 (1974); and *Erznoznik v. City of Jacksonville*, 422 U.S. 205 (1975). But compare contrary rulings in *Times Film Corp. v. City of Chicago*, 365 U.S. 43 (1961); *Paris Adult Theatre I v. Slaton*, 413 U.S. 49 (1973); *Young v. American Mini Theaters*, 427 U.S. 50 (1976); and *City of Renton v. Playtime Theatres, Inc.*, 475 U.S. 41 (1986). For further discussion, see chapter 2.

21. *Thornhill v. Alabama*, 310 U.S. 102 (1940).

22. See *Cantwell v. Connecticut*, 310 U.S. 296 (1940); *Douglas v. City of Jeanette*, 319 U.S. 157 (1943); *Jones v. Opelika*, 319 U.S. 103 (1943); *Murdock v. Pennsylvania*, 319 U.S. 105 (1943); and *Follet v. Town of McCormick*, 321 U.S. 573 (1944).

23. See and compare *Minersville School District v. Gobitus*, 310 U.S. 586 (1940), with *West Virginia Board of Education v. Barnette*, 319 U.S. 624 (1944).

24. *Bridges v. California*, 314 U.S. 252 (1941); *Pennekamp v. Florida*, 328 U.S. 331 (1946); *Craig v. Harney*, 331 U.S. 367 (1947) (contempt-of-court citations for publications concerning pending trials); and *Terminiello v. Chicago*, 337 U.S. 1 (1949) (conviction for public speech).

25. *Jones v. Opelika*, 316 U.S. 584, 608 (1942) (C. J. Stone, dissenting), adopted on rehearing in *Jones v. Opelika*, 319 U.S. 103 (1943).

26. See *Bridges v. California*, 314 U.S. 252, 295 (1941); *Craig v. Harney*, 331 U.S. 367, 391 (1947); and *Kovacs v. Cooper*, 336 U.S. 77, 96 (1949).

27. *Dennis v. United States*, 341 U.S. 494 (1951).

28. *Communist Party of the United States v. Subversive Activities Control Board (SACB)*, 367 U.S. 1 (1961).

29. *Dennis*, however, was presaged by Chief Justice Vinson's opinion in *American Communications Association v. Douds*, 339 U.S. 382 (1940), upholding a requirement for the filing on non-Communist affidavits in the Labor-Management Relations Act.

30. See also Justice Hugo LaFayette Black, *A Constitutional Faith* (New York: Knopf, 1968), 43–63.

31. *Yates v. United States*, 354 U.S. 178 (1957).

32. *Barenblatt v. United States*, 360 U.S. 109 (1959).

33. *Scales v. United States*, 367 U.S. 203 (1961).

34. *Communist Party of the United States v. Subversive Activities Control Board (SACB)*, 367 U.S. 1 (1961).

35. *Deutch v. United States*, 367 U.S. 456 (1961).

36. *Brandenburg v. Ohio*, 395 U.S. 444 (1969).

37. For further discussion, see Frank Strong, "Fifty Years of 'Clear and Present Danger'" in Philip Kurland, ed., *The Supreme Court Review* (Chicago: University of Chicago Press, 1969), 431.

38. Black, *A Constitutional Faith*, 45. See also Edmund Cahn, "Justice Black and First Amendment 'Absolutes': A Public Interview," 37 *New York University Law Review* 549 (1962).

39. See, for example, Thomas I. Emerson, *The System of Freedom of Expression* (New York: Random House, 1970); and Robert McKay, "The Preference for Freedom," 34 *New York University Law Review* 1182 (1959). For defenses of balancing, see Walter Berns, *The First Amendment and the Future of American Democracy* (New York: Basic Books, 1976); and Walter Berns, *Freedom, Virtue and the First Amendment* (Baton Rouge: Louisiana State University Press, 1957).

40. See, for example, Justice William J. Brennan Jr., "The Supreme Court and the Meiklejohn Interpretation of the First Amendment," 79 *Harvard Law Review* 1 (1965); Alexander Meiklejohn, "The First Amendment Is an Absolute," in Philip Kurland, ed., *The Supreme Court Review* (Chicago: University of Chicago Press, 1961), 245; and Alexander Meiklejohn, *Political Freedom* (New York: Harper & Row, 1948).

41. *Chaplinsky v. New Hampshire*, 315 U.S. 568 (1942).

42. See *Associated Press v. United States*, 326 U.S. 1 (1945); *Giboney v. Empire Storage & Ice Co.*, 336 U.S. 499 (1949); *Lorain Journal Co. v. United States*, 342 U.S. 143 (1951); *Eastern Railroad Presidents Conference et al. v.*

Noerr Motor Freight, Inc., 365 U.S. 127 (1961); and *United Mine Workers of America v. Pennington*, 381 U.S. 657 (1965).

43. See *Harper & Row v. Nation Enterprises*, 471 U.S. 539 (1985); and *Eldred v. Ashcroft*, 537 U.S. 186 (2003).

44. See, for example, Richard Dooling, *Blue Streak: Swearing, Free Speech, and Sexual Harassment* (New York: Random House, 1996).

45. See *Beard v. Banks*, 548 U.S. 521 (2006); and *Turner v. Safley*, 482 U.S. 78 (1987). See also *Procunier v. Martinez*, 416 U.S. 396 (1974).

46. See, for example, *United Public Workers of America v. Mitchell*, 330 U.S. 75 (1947) (upholding restrictions on public employees' expression under the Hatch Act); *United States Civil Service Commission v. National Association of Letter Carriers*, 413 U.S. 548 (1973); *Abood v. District Board of Education*, 431 U.S. 209 (1977); *Snepp v. United States*, 444 U.S. 507 (1980); and *Communications Workers of America v. Beck*, 487 U.S. 735 (1988). But see also rulings upholding First Amendment claims in *Pickering v. Board of Education of Township High School*, 391 U.S. 563 (1968); *Elrod v. Burns*, 427 U.S. 347 (1976); *Branti v. Finkel*, 445 U.S. 507 (1980); *Rankin v. McPherson*, 483 U.S. 378 (1987); *Rutan v. Republican Party of Illinois*, 497 U.S. 62 (1990); and *United States v. National Treasury Employees Union*, 513 U.S. 432 (1995).

47. See *Regan v. Taxation With Representation*, 461 U.S. 540 (1983); *Rust v. Sullivan*, 500 U.S. 173 (1991); *Rosenberger v. Rector and Visitors of the University of Virginia*, 515 U.S. 819 (1995); *National Endowment for the Arts v. Finley*, 524 U.S. 569 (1998); *Rumsfeld v. Forum for Academic and Institutional Rights*, 546 U.S. 807 (2006); *Pleasant Grove City v. Summum*, 129 S. Ct. 1125 (2007). But compare decisions upholding First Amendment claims in *Perry v. Sindermann*, 408 U.S. 503 (1972); *FCC v. League of Women Voters of California*, 468 U.S. 364 (1984); *Arkansas Writers' Project, Inc. v. Ragland*, 481 U.S. 221 (1987); *Legal Services Corporation v. Velazquez*, 351 U.S. 533 (2001); *Nebraska Cattlemen Inc. v. Livestock Marketing Association*, 468 U.S. 364 (2005); and *Johanns v. Livestock Marketing Association*, 481 U.S. 221 (2005).

48. For a further discussion see chapter 5 and, generally, Jamin H. Raskin, *We the Students: Supreme Court Decisions for and about Students*, second edition (Washington, D.C.: CQ Press, 2003).

49. See *Breard v. City of Alexandria*, 341 U.S. 622 (1951); *Public Utilities Commission v. Pollock*, 343 U.S. 451 (1952); *Rowan v. United States Post Office*, 397 U.S. 728 (1970); *Lehman v. City of Shaker Heights*, 418 U.S. 298 (1974); *Ohralik v. Ohio State Bar Association*, 436 U.S. 447 (1978); and *Federal Communications Commission v. Pacifica Foundation*, 438 U.S. 530 (1978). But the Court sustained First Amendment claims in *Kunz v. New York*, 340 U.S. 290 (1951); *Cohen v. California*, 403 U.S. 15 (1971); *Hess v.*

Indiana, 414 U.S. 105 (1973); *Erznoznik v. City of Jacksonville*, 422 U.S. 205 (1975); *Givhan v. Western Line Consolidated School District*, 439 U.S. 410 (1979); and *Consolidated Edison Co. v. Public Service Commission*, 447 U.S. 530 (1980).

50. See *Kovacs v. Cooper*, 336 U.S. 77 (1949); *Grayned v. City of Rockford*, 408 U.S. 104 (1972); *Heffron v. International Society for Krishna Consciousness*, 452 U.S. 640 (1981); *City of Renton v. Playtime Theatres, Inc.*, 475 U.S. 41 (1986); *Frisby v. Schultz*, 487 U.S. 474 (1988); *Ward v. Rock Against Racism*, 491 U.S. 781 (1989); *United States v. Kokinda*, 497 U.S. 720 (1990); *Madsen v. Women's Health Center, Inc.*, 512 U.S. 753 (1997); *Hill v. Colorado*, 530 U.S. 703 (2000); and *Thomas v. Chicago Park District*, 534 U.S. 316 (2001). However, the Court upheld First Amendment claims over time, place, and manner regulations in *Lovell v. City of Griffin*, 303 U.S. 444 (1938); *Schneider v. New Jersey*, 308 U.S. 147 (1939); *Martin v. City of Struthers*, 319 U.S. 141 (1943); *Police Department of City of Chicago v. Mosely*, 408 U.S. 92 (1972); *Consolidated Edison Co. v. Public Service Commission*, 447 U.S. 530 (1980); *Schad v. Mount Ephraim*, 452 U.S. 61 (1981); *United States v. Grace*, 461 U.S. 171 (1983); and *City of Ladue v. Gilleo*, 512 U.S. 43 (1994). See also *Schenck v. Pro-Choice Network of Western New York*, 519 U.S. 357 (1997), upholding and rejecting First Amendment claims in part.

51. See *Kovacs v. Cooper*, 336 U.S. 77 (1949); *Grayned v. City of Rockford*, 408 U.S. 104 (1972); and *Ward v. Rock Against Racism*, 491 U.S. 781 (1989). But compare *Saia v. New York*, 334 U.S. 558 (1948), upholding First Amendment claims.

52. See, for example, Pierre Schlag, "An Attack on Categorical Approaches to Freedom of the Speech," 30 *UCLA Law Review* 671 (1983).

53. *R. A. V. v. City of St. Paul, Minnesota*, 505 U.S. 377 (1992). See also *Virginia v. Black*, 538 U.S. 343 (2003), and the discussion in chapter 5.

54. For further discussion, see, for example, Ronald K. L. Collins and David M. Skover, *The Death of Discourse*, second edition (Durham: Carolina Academic Press, 2005), 3–7 (on commercial speech); Catharine MacKinnon, *Only Words* (Cambridge, Mass.: Harvard University Press, 1993) (on pornography); and Mari J. Matsuda et al., *Words That Wound: Critical Race Theory, Assaultive Speech, and the First Amendment* (Boulder, Colo.: Westview Press, 1993).

Chapter 2

1. *Regina v. Hicklin*, L.R. 2 Q.B. 360 (1868). See also *Ex parte Jackson*, 96 U.S. 727 (1877) (discussing the First Amendment in *dicta* when uphold-

ing the Comstock Act and Congress's power to establish the post office and to regulate the mails).

2. *Butler v. Michigan,* 352 U.S. 380 (1957).

3. *Roth v. United States* and *Alberts v. California,* 354 U.S. 476 (1957).

4. *Kingsley International Corporation v. Regents of the University of New York,* 360 U.S. 684 (1959).

5. *Manual Enterprises, Inc. v. Day,* 370 U.S. 478 (1962).

6. *Jacobellis v. State of Ohio,* 378 U.S. 184 (1964).

7. *A Book Named "John Cleland's Memoirs of a Woman of Pleasure" v. Massachusetts,* 383 U.S. 413 (1966).

8. *Ginzburg v. United States,* 383 U.S. 463 (1966).

9. *Ginsberg v. New York,* 390 U.S. 629 (1968). See also *Virginia v. American Booksellers Association, Inc.,* 484 U.S. 383 (1988) (remanding a case challenging a Virginia statute making it unlawful for any person "to knowingly display for commercial purposes in a manner whereby juveniles may examine" sexual or sadomasochistic material that is harmful to juveniles).

10. See, for example, *Kingsley Books v. Brown,* 354 U.S. 436 (1957) (held that a city may get injunction against sale of indecent books with appeal and trial within two days); *Times Film Corporation v. City of Chicago,* 365 U.S. 43 (1961) (no absolute right to exhibit, even once, any and every kind of film; no prior censorship of permit system); *Miskin v. New York,* 383 U.S. 502 (1966) (denied a First Amendment challenge to a conviction under New York's law of a book distributor for publishing allegedly obscene books on sadism and masochism); *Heller v. New York,* 413 U.S. 483 (1973) (held that since a judge viewed the entire film before issuing a warrant for its seizure, no adversary hearing prior to the seizure was required); *Hamling v. United States,* 418 U.S. 87 (1974) (rejected a First Amendment challenge to a federal statute banning the mailing of obscene material for failing to provide "adequate notice" and to meet the "community standards" guidelines laid out in *Miller v. California,* 413 U.S. 15 [1973]); *Ward v. Illinois,* 431 U.S. 767 (1977) (denied a First Amendment claim that an Illinois obscenity statute was overly broad); *Brockett v. Spokane Arcades, Inc.,* 472 U.S. 491 (1985) (rejected a First Amendment challenge to a Washington law dealing with obscenity and "moral lewdness" in materials); and *Alexander v. United States,* 509 U.S. 344 (1993) (rejected a First Amendment claim that RICO's forfeiture provisions constituted a prior restraint).

However, the Court sustained First Amendment claims over federal, state, or local regulations in a number of other cases. See, for example, *Winters v. New York,* 333 U.S. 507 (1948) (held that a state statute prohibiting the publication of violent materials was overly vague and ran afoul of the First Amendment); *Bantam Books, Inc. v. Sullivan,* 372 U.S. 58 (1963) (held that the Rhode Island Committee on Morality constituted prior restraint in providing no hearing on books banned for youths); *A Quantity of Copies of Books v. Kansas*, 378 US 205 (1964) (found that procedure for impoundment of books was unconstitutional); *Freedman v. Maryland*, 380 U.S. 51 (1965) (held that the state motion picture censorship statute failed to provide adequate safeguards against undue repression of speech); *Redrup v. New York*, 386 U.S. 767 (1967) (held that the conviction of a newsstand clerk for selling two "obscene" paperback books violated the First Amendment); *Teitel Film Corporation v. Cusack*, 390 U.S. 139 (1968) (held that the censorship board for review of films was unconstitutional, where fifty days passed before completion of administrative process and no provision was made for prompt judicial decision); *Blount v. Rizzi*, 400 U.S. 410 (1971) (held that a federal statute authorizing the postmaster general to censor allegedly obscene mailings lacked adequate safeguards to ensure First Amendment freedom of expression); *Rabe v. Washington*, 405 U.S. 313 (1972) (held the state's obscenity statute, proscribing showing of pictures at a drive-in, which could be shown in adult theaters, was unconstitutionally vague); *Roaden v. Kentucky*, 413 U.S. 496 (1973) (holding the seizure of a film in public distribution without warrant was prior restraint and violated Fourth Amendment); *Hamling v. United States*, 418 U.S. 87 (1974) (rejecting a First Amendment challenge to a federal statute banning the mailing of obscene material for failing to provide "adequate notice" and to meet the "community standards" guidelines laid out in *Miller v. California*, 413 U.S. 15 [1973]); *Southern Promotions, Ltd. v. Conrad*, 420 U.S. 546 (1975) (held denial of city-leased theater for the theatrical production of *Hair* was a prior restraint because it was imposed without procedural safeguards); *McKinney v. Alabama*, 424 U.S. 669 (1976) (upholding a First Amendment claim in the prosecution of a bookseller charged with selling "obscene mailable matter" who at trial was not permitted to contest the alleged obscenity of the magazines sold in the store); *Vance v. Universal Amusement Co.*, 445 U.S. 308 (1980) (struck down as prior restraint restriction on an exhibition of "obscene motion pictures"); *Fort Wayne Books, Inc. v. Indiana*, 489 U.S. 46 (1989) (held that the First Amendment was violated by the seizure, under the RICO statute, of an adult bookstore and its contents); *Sable Communications of California v. Federal Communications Commission*, 492 U.S. 115 (1989) (held that a California law banning indecent and obscene telephone messages violated the First Amendment).

11. *Stanley v. Georgia*, 394 U.S. 561 (1969).

12. See *Hoyt v. Minnesota*, 399 U.S. 524 (1970); *Cain v. Kentucky*, 387 U.S. 319 (1970); and *Walker v. Ohio*, 398 U.S. 434 (1970).

13. *Miller v. California*, 413 U.S. 15 (1973).

14. *Paris Adult Theatre I v. Slaton*, 413 U.S. 49 (1973).

15. *United States v. 37-Photographs*, 402 U.S. 363 (1971).

16. *United States v. 12 200-Ft. Reels of Super 8-mm Film*, 413 U.S. 123 (1973). See also *Hamling v. United States*, 418 U.S. 87 (1974) (rejecting a First Amendment challenge to a federal statute banning the mailing of obscene material for failing to provide "adequate notice" and to meet the "community standards" test set forth in *Miller v. California*, 413 U.S. 15 [1973]).

17. See, for example, *Novick, Haim and Unique Specialities, Inc. v. U.S. District Court*, 423 U.S. 911 (1975).

18. *Jenkins v. Georgia*, 413 U.S. 496 (1973). However, in *Smith v. United States*, 431 U.S. 291 (1977), the Court held that juries may determine "community standards" in federal prosecutions.

19. *Pinkus v. United States*, 436 U.S. 293 (1978).

20. *Pope v. Illinois*, 481 U.S. 497 (1987).

21. *Rowan v. U.S. Post Office Department*, 397 U.S. 728 (1970), sustained a federal obscenity statute allowing individuals to request that the post office not deliver unsolicited mailings to their homes of materials they find offensive. *United States v. Reidel*, 402 U.S. 351 (1971), upheld a federal obscenity statute prohibiting the mailing of certain pornographic materials.

22. *New York v. Ferber*, 458 U.S. 747 (1982).

23. *Osborne v. Ohio*, 495 U.S. 103 (1990).

24. *Ashcroft v. Free Speech Coalition*, 534 U.S. 234 (2002).

25. Justice O'Connor, joined by Chief Justice Rehnquist and Justice Scalia, dissented and would have upheld the section of CPPA banning pornographic depictions that "appear to be" of minors so long as it was not applied to youthful-adult pornography.

26. *Ashcroft v. American Civil Liberties Union*, 542 U.S. 656 (2004).

27. *Reno v. American Civil Liberties Union*, 521 U.S. 844 (1997).

28. *Ashcroft v. American Civil Liberties Union*, 535 U.S. 564 (2002).

29. See *American Civil Liberties Union v. Mukasey*, 534 F.3d 181 (2008), *cert.* denied in *Mukasey v. American Civil Liberties Union*, 129 S. Ct. 1032 (2009).

30. *United States v. American Library Association*, 539 U.S. 126 (2003).

31. *United States v. Williams*, 128 S. Ct. 1830 (2008).

32. See, for example, *Cox Broadcasting Company v. Cohn*, 420 U.S. 469 (1975); *Smith v. Daily Mail Publishing Company*, 443 U.S. 97 (1979); and *Globe Newspaper Company v. Superior Court for the County of Norfolk*, 457 U.S. 596 (1982).

33. See *Joseph Burstyn v. Wilson*, 343 U.S. 495 (1952) (striking down New York's blasphemy law as an unconstitutional prior restraint), and, generally, Laura Wittern-Keller and Raymond Haberski, *The Miracle Case: Film Censorship and the Supreme Court* (Lawrence: University of Kansas Press, 2008); Leonard W. Levi, *Blasphemy: Verbal Offense against the Sacred, from Moses*

to *Salman Rushdie* (Chapel Hill: University of North Carolina Press, 1995); and Alan Dershowitz, *Blasphemy: How the Religious Right Is Hijacking the Declaration of Independence* (New York: Wiley, 2008). Some states, however, still have laws punishing blasphemy, such as Massachusetts, Michigan, Oklahoma, Mississippi, and North Carolina; see David Hudson Jr., "Curses! Blasphemy, Profanity Laws Still on the Books," firstamendmentcenter .org/analysis.aspx?id = 21938 (accessed September 8, 2009).

34. See *Cohen v. California*, 403 U.S. 15 (1971) (discussed later in the chapter).

35. See *Erznoznik v. City of Jacksonville*, 422 U.S. 205 (1975) (striking down an ordinance making it a public nuisance to show any motion picture containing nudity in a drive-in theater where the screen was visible from a public street). See also *Southeastern Promotions v. Conrad*, 420 U.S. 546 (1975) (holding that the denial of the use of a municipal auditorium for the production of *Hair*—a play involving nudity—constituted a prior restraint).

36. See *Sable Communications of California v. Federal Communications Commission*, 492 U.S. 115 (1989) (striking down a 1988 federal statute banning indecent telephone "dial-a-porn" services).

37. See, for example, *United States v. Playboy Entertainment Group, Inc.*, 529 U.S. 803 (2000); and *Denver Area Education Telecommunications Consortium, Inc. v. Federal Communications Commission*, 518 U.S. 727 (1996) (striking down a similar requirement, under the Cable Television Consumer Protection Act of 1992, that cable companies block access to sexually explicit materials).

38. See *Reno v. American Civil Liberties Union*, 521 U.S. 844 (1997) (discussed later in the chapter).

39. See, for example, *Barnes v. Glen Theatre Inc.*, 501 U.S. 560 (1991); and *City of Erie v. Pap's A. M.*, 529 U.S. 277 (2000) (discussed later in the chapter).

40. See *Federal Communications Commission v. Pacifica Foundation*, 438 U.S. 726 (1978) (discussed later in the chapter), and Lili Levi, *The FCC's Regulation of Indecency*, First Reports, vol. 7, no. 1 (Washington, D.C.: First Amendment Center, April 2008).

41. See *National Endowment for the Arts v. Finley*, 524 U.S. 569 (1998) (upholding a 1990 amendment to the National Endowment for the Arts Act, requiring the NEA to take "general standards of decency" into account when awarding grants to artists).

42. See, for example, *Bethel School District No. 403 v. Fraser*, 478 U.S. 675 (1986) (discussed further in chapter 5).

43. *Cohen v. California*, 403 U.S. 15 (1971).

44. *Rowan v. U.S Post Office Department*, 397 U.S. 728 (1970).

45. *Erznoznik v. City of Jacksonville*, 422 U.S. 205 (1975).

46. *Federal Communications Commission v. Pacifica Foundation*, 438 U.S. 726 (1978).

47. See also *Lehman v. Shaker Heights*, 418 U.S. 298 (1974) (holding that bus placards are not public forums protected by the First Amendment).

48. 18 U.S.C. Sec. 1464. For a further discussion, see Lili Levi, *The FCC's Regulation of Indecency*, First Reports, vol. 7, no. 1 (Washington, D.C.: First Amendment Center, April 2008).

49. *Federal Communications Commission v. Fox Television Stations*, 129 S. Ct. 1800 (2009).

50. See, for example, *Wilkinson v. Jones*, 480 U.S. 926 (1987) (affirming without a written opinion a lower court ruling striking down Utah's statute restricting cable telecasts of "indecent" images); *Denver Area Telecommunications Consortium v. Federal Communications Commission*, 518 U.S. 727 (1996) (striking down two provisions restricting the programming of "indecent material" in the Cable Television Consumer Protection and Competition Act of 1992); and *United States v. Playboy Enterprises Group, Inc.*, 529 U.S. 803 (2000) (striking down provisions of the Telecommunications Act of 1966 requiring cable operators providing sexually oriented programming to scramble those channels or limit transmissions to hours between 10 p.m. and 6 a.m.).

51. *Young v. American Mini Theatres*, 427 U.S. 50 (1976).

52. *Renton v. Playtime Theatres*, 475 U.S. 41 (1986). *Areara v. Cloud Books, Inc.*, 478 U.S. 697 (1986), also allowed the closing of a bookstore where its premises were used for the purpose of soliciting prostitution, and *City of Los Angeles v. Alameda Books, Inc.*, 535 U.S. 425 (2002), upheld a zoning ordinance barring more than one adult establishment from operating at the same location. But see also *City of Littleton v. Z. J. Gifts D-4, L.L.C.*, 541 U.S. 774 (2004) (reaffirming that ordinances requiring the licensing of adult businesses must provide access to judicial review and a prompt judicial decision); and *Boos v. Barry*, 485 U.S. 312 (1988) (striking down a law barring a sign within five hundred feet of a foreign embassy as not content neutral and rejecting the claim that the "emotive impact" of such expression had a "secondary effect" on its audience).

53. *California v. La Rue*, 409 U.S. 109 (1972).

54. *New York State Liquor Authority v. Bellanca*, 452 U.S. 714 (1981); reaffirmed in *City of Newport, Kentucky v. Iacobucci*, 479 U.S. 92 (1986).

55. See *Schad v. Borough of Mount Ephraim*, 452 U.S. 61 (1981). In *Larkin v. Grendel's Den, Inc.*, 459 U.S. 116 (1982), the Court struck down a Massachusetts statute giving churches the power to veto applications for liquor licenses, including for adult bars.

56. *Barnes v. Glen Theatre*, 501 U.S. 560 (1991).

57. Chief Justice Rehnquist relied on and applied the four-prong test set forth in *United States v. O'Brien*, 391 U.S. 367 (1968).

58. *City of Erie v. Pap's A. M.*, 529 U.S. 277 (2000).

59. *Reno v. American Civil Liberties Union*, 521 U.S. 844 (1997).

60. *Ashcroft v. Free Speech Coalition*, 534 U.S. 234 (2002).

61. *United States v. American Library Association*, 539 U.S. 126 (2003).

Chapter 3

1. *New York Times Co. v. Sullivan*, 376 U.S. 254 (1964), further discussed in the chapter.

2. *Beauharnais v. Illinois*, 343 U.S. 250 (1952).

3. See *Ashton v. Kentucky*, 384 U.S. 195 (1966).

4. *R.A.V. v. City of St. Paul*, 505 U.S. 377 (1992), which is further discussed in chapter 5. See also *Smith v. Collin*, 436 U.S. 953 (1978), in which dissenting Justices Blackmun and Rehnquist underscore that "*Beauharnais* has never been overruled or formally limited in any way."

5. But see *Hutchinson v. Proxmire*, 443 U.S. 111 (1979).

6. See *Gravel v. United States*, 408 U.S. 606 (1972); *United States v. Johnson*, 169 (1966); *United States v. Brewster*, 408 U.S. 501 (1972); *Eastland v. United States Servicemen's Fund*, 421 U.S. 491 (1975); and *United States v. Helstoski*, 442 U.S. 477 (1979). But see also *Drombrowski v. Eastland*, 387 U.S. 82 (1967); and *Doe v. McMillan*, 412 U.S. 306 (1973).

7. *New York Times Co. v. Sullivan*, 376 U.S. 254 (1964).

8. *St. Amant v. Thompson*, 390 U.S. 727 (1968).

9. *Rosenblatt v. Baer*, 383 U.S. 75 (1966).

10. *Associated Press v. Walker*, 388 U.S. 130 (1967).

11. *Curtis Publishing Company v. Butts*, 388 U.S. 130 (1967).

12. See *Greenbelt Corp. v. Bresler*, 398 U.S. 6 (1970) (held that use of the term "blackmail" when characterizing the conduct of a real estate developer, who was deemed to be a public figure, seeking zoning variances was not libel); *Monitor Patriot Co. v. Roy*, 401 U.S. 265 (1971) (held that candidates for elective office were "public officials" or "public figures" subject to actual malice test); and *Rosenbloom v. Metromedia*, 403 U.S. 29 (1971) (held that a distributor of nudist magazines, who was called a "smut peddler," but was later acquitted of obscenity charges, had to prove actual malice).

13. *Gertz v. Robert Welch, Inc.*, 428 U.S. 323 (1974).

14. *Time, Inc. v. Firestone*, 424 U.S. 448 (1976).

15. See also *Wolston v. Reader's Digest*, 443 U.S. 157 (1979), holding that an alleged KGB spy was not a public figure.

16. *Philadelphia Newspapers, Inc. v. Hepps*, 475 U.S. 767 (1986).

17. *Milkovich v. Lorain Journal Co.*, 497 U.S. 1 (1990).
18. *Philadelphia Newspapers, Inc. v. Hepps*, 475 U.S. 767 (1986).
19. See, for example, *Anderson v. Liberty Lobby*, 477 U.S. 242 (1986), holding that libel suits should go only if there is clear and convincing evidence of actual malice.
20. *Herbert v. Lando*, 441 U.S. 153 (1979).
21. *Philadelphia Newspapers, Inc. v. Hepps*, 475 U.S. 767 (1986).
22. *Masson v. The New Yorker Magazine*, 501 U.S. 496 (1991).
23. See also *Bose Corporation v. Consumers Union*, 466 U.S. 485 (1984), holding that the actual malice test applies in a libel suit against a consumer magazine for a review of loudspeakers; and *Dun & Bradstreet, Inc. v. Greenmoss Builders, Inc.*, 472 U.S. 749 (1985), holding that a contractor need not prove actual malice in a suit against a credit reporting agency for issuing false credit reports to a bank.
24. See *Hustler Magazine v. Falwell*, 485 U.S. 46 (1988), holding that a public figure was not entitled to recovering damages for emotional distress due to an advertisement parody.
25. See *Keeton v. Hustler Magazine*, 465 U.S. 770 (1984).
26. See William Prosser, "Privacy," 48 *California Law Review* 383 (1960).
27. *Time, Inc. v. Hill*, 385 U.S. 374 (1967).
28. *Cantrell v. Forest City Publishing Company*, 419 U.S. 245 (1974).
29. *Cox Broadcasting Corporation v. Cohn*, 420 U.S. 469 (1975).
30. *The Florida Star v. B. J. F.*, 491 U.S. 524 (1989). See also *Globe Newspaper Company v. Superior Court for the County of Norfolk*, 457 U.S. 596 (1982), striking down a state statute excluding the press and public from the courtroom in cases involving the testimony of victims under the age of eighteen.
31. See *Hustler Magazine v. Falwell*, 485 U.S. 46 (1988).
32. *Zacchini v. Scripps-Howard Broadcasting Corporation*, 433 U.S. 562 (1977).

Chapter 4

1. In a major ruling in *Citizens United v. Federal Election Commission*, 130 S. Ct. 876 (2010), the Roberts Court overturned two precedents and held that Congress could not bar corporations' independent expenditures for candidates for federal election, but did so without mentioning the commercial speech doctrine and dealt with the matter as First Amendment for expression in elections.
2. *Valentine v. Chrestensen*, 316 U.S. 52 (1942). *Valentine* was later

overruled in *Virginia State Board of Pharmacy v. Virginia Citizens Consumer Council, Inc.*, 425 U.S. 748 (1976), which is discussed later in this chapter.

3. *New York Times v. Sullivan*, 376 U.S. 254 (1964), discussed in more detail in chapter 3.

4. *Pittsburgh Press v. Pittsburgh Commission on Human Rights*, 413 U.S. 376 (1973).

5. *Bigelow v. Virginia*, 421 U.S. 809 (1975).

6. *Roe v. Wade*, 410 U.S. 113 (1973).

7. *Posadas de Puerto Rico Associates v. Tourism Company of Puerto Rico*, 479 U.S. 328 (1986).

8. *Bates v. State Bar of Arizona*, 433 U.S. 350 (1977).

9. *In re Primus*, 436 U.S. 412 (1978).

10. *Ohralik v. Ohio State Bar Association*, 436 U.S. 447 (1978).

11. *In re R. M. J.*, 455 U.S. 191 (1982).

12. *Zauderer v. Office of Disciplinary Counsel of Supreme Court of Ohio*, 471 U.S. 626 (1985).

13. See *Shapero v. Kentucky Bar Association*, 486 U.S. 466 (1988), and *Peel v. Attorney Disciplinary Commission of Illinois*, 496 U.S. 91 (1990)—both upholding First Amendment claims. However, writing for a bare majority in *Florida Bar Association v. Went for It, Inc.*, 515 U.S. 618 (1995), Justice O'Connor (1981–2006) upheld Florida's prohibition on lawyers making written solicitations to victims and victims' relatives within thirty days of an accident or natural disaster, on concluding that the government's interests in the restriction met the test set forth in *Central Hudson Gas & Electric Corp. v. Public Service Commission of New York*, 446 U.S. 557 (1980) (further discussed in this chapter). By contrast, Justices Stevens, Kennedy, Souter, and Ginsburg strongly disagreed with the majority's analysis and failure to recognize First Amendment protection for attorney advertising.

14. See *Carey v. Population Services International*, 431 U.S. 678 (1978), and *Bolger v. Youngs Drug Products Corp.*, 463 U.S. 60 (1983).

15. See *Central Hudson Gas & Electric Corp. v. Public Service Commission of New York*, 447 U.S. 557 (1980) (discussed later in this chapter); *Consolidated Edison Co. Public Service Commission*, 447 U.S. 530 (1980); and *Pacific Gas & Electric Co. v. Public Utilities Commission*, 475 U.S. 1 (1986), holding that governments may not force a utility company to include in its newsletters materials by third parties.

16. See *Linmark Associates, Inc. v. Township of Willingboro*, 431 U.S. 85 (1985).

17. See *Metro Media, Inc. v. City of San Diego*, 453 U.S. 490 (1981). See also *Lorillard Tobacco Co. v. Reilly*, 533 U.S. 535 (2001) (holding federal preemption of state tobacco regulations).

18. See *City of Cincinnati v. Discovery Network*, 507 U.S. 410 (1993).

19. See *Bolger v. Youngs Drug Products Corp.*, 463 U.S. 60 (1983); and *Shapero v. Kentucky Bar Association*, 486 U.S. 466 (1988). But compare *Florida Bar Association v. Went for It, Inc.*, 515 U.S. 618 (1995).

20. See *Edenfield v. Fane*, 507 U.S. 761 (1993); and *Ibanez v. Florida Department of Professional Regulation*, 512 U.S. 136 (1994).

21. See *Thompson v. Western States Medical Central*, 535 U.S. 357 (2002).

22. *Virginia State Board of Pharmacy v. Virginia Citizen Consumer Council*, 425 U.S. 748 (1976).

23. *Board of Trustees of the State of New York v. Fox*, 492 U.S. 469, 477 (1989), quoting *Ohralik v. Ohio State Bar Association*, 436 U.S. 447, 456 (1978).

24. *Friedman v. Rogers*, 440 U.S. 1 (1979).

25. *Board of Trustees of the State University of New York v. Fox*, 492 U.S. 469 (1989).

26. See, for example, *Columbia Broadcasting System v. Democratic National Committee*, 412 U.S. 94 (1973), and *City Council of Los Angeles v. Taxpayers for Vincent*, 466 U.S. 789 (1984).

27. *United States v. Edge Broadcasting Co.*, 509 U.S. 418 (1993).

28. *Village of Hoffman Estates v. Flipside*, 455 U.S. 489 (1982).

29. See and compare *Glickman v. Wileman Brothers & Elliott, Inc.*, 521 U.S. 457 (1997), upholding a federal requirement requiring fruit producers to contribute to generic ads for fruit in certain markets, with *United States v. United Foods*, 533 U.S. 405 (2001), striking down a federal statute mandating that mushroom handlers pay a fee that was used to fund ads promoting the sale of mushrooms.

30. See and compare *Posadas de Puerto Rico Associates v. Tourism Company of Puerto Rico.*, 479 U.S. 328 (1986), upholding a ban on casino advertising, with *Greater New Orleans Broadcasting Association v. United States*, 537 U.S. 173 (1999), upholding First Amendment claims to protection for broadcasting ads for gambling.

31. See and compare *Murdock v. Pennsylvania*, 319 U.S. 105 (1943), and *Schaumburg v. Citizens for a Better Environment*, 444 U.S. 620 (1980) (both upholding First Amendment claims) with *Breard v. City of Alexandria*, 341 U.S. 622 (1951).

32. See, for example, *City Council of Los Angeles v. Taxpayers for Vincent*, 466 U.S. 789 (1984), and *Pacific Gas & Electric Co. v. Public Utilities Commission*, 475 U.S. 1 (1986).

33. *Central Hudson Gas & Electric Corp. v. Public Service Commission of New York*, 447 U.S. 557 (1980).

34. See, for example, *Posadas de Puerto Rico Associates v. Tourism Company of Puerto Rico*, 479 U.S. 328 (1986); *United States v. Edge Broadcasting*

Company, 509 U.S. 418 (1993); and *Florida Bar Association v. Went For It, Inc.*, 515 U.S. 618 (1995).

35. See, for example, *Rubin v. Coors Brewing Co.*, 514 U.S. 476 (1995); *Greater New Orleans Broadcasting Association v. United States*, 527 U.S. 173 (1999); and *Lorillard Tobacco Co. v. Reilly*, 533 U.S. 525 (2001).

36. *Lorillard Tobacco Co. v. Reilly*, 533 U.S. 525, 572 (2001) (J. Thomas, concurring). See also Justice Thomas's concurring opinion in *44 Liquormart, Inc. v. Rhode Island*, 517 U.S. 484, 518–528 (1996).

37. *Posadas de Puerto Rico Associates v. Tourism Company of Puerto Rico*, 479 U.S. 328 (1986).

38. *Meyer v. Grant*, 486 U.S. 414 (1988).

39. *Rubin v. Coors Brewing Company*, 514 U.S. 476 (1995).

40. *44 Liquormart v. Rhode Island*, 517 U.S. 484 (1996).

41. *Lorillard Tobacco Company v. Reilly*, 533 U.S. 525 (2001).

42. *Thompson v. Western States Medical Center*, 535 U.S. 357 (2002).

43. See *Los Angeles Police Department v. United Reporting Publishing Corporation*, 528 U.S. 32 (1999).

44. See, for example, *Johanns v. Livestock Marketing Association*, 544 U.S. 550 (2005), with Justices Stevens, Kennedy, and Souter dissenting. See also *Glickman v. Wileman Brothers & Elliott, Inc.*, 521 U.S. 457 (1997), and compare *United States v. United Foods*, 533 U.S. 405 (2001).

Chapter 5

1. *Chaplinsky v. New Hampshire*, 315 U.S. 568 (1942).

2. The Court, however, upheld an injunction against the intimidation of a company's employees by labor pickets with the epithet "scab" in *Youngdahl v. Rainfair, Inc.*, 355 U.S. 131 (1957). But subsequently the Court ruled that the use of "scab" and other such epithets during labor disputes are protected expression; see *Letter Carriers v. Austin*, 418 U.S. 264 (1974), and *Linn v. United Plant Guard Workers*, 383 U.S. 53 (1966).

3. Hostile audiences and provocative speech is discussed later in this chapter, but see *Chaplinsky v. New Hampshire*, 315 U.S. 568 (1942), and *Feiner v. New York*, 340 U.S. 315 (1951) (denying a First Amendment claim to protection for street speech before a hostile audience); and compare *Terminiello v. Chicago*, 357 U.S. 1 (1949) (upholding a First Amendment claim for a provocative speech on a public street before a hostile audience).

4. For a further discussion, see Stephen W. Gard, "Fighting Words as Free Speech," 58 *Washington University Law Quarterly* 531 (1980). But see also Kent Greenawalt, *Fighting Words* (Princeton, N.J.: Princeton University Press, 1996).

5. *Gooding v. Wilson*, 405 U.S. 518 (1972). See also *Lucas v. Arkansas*, 416 U.S. 919 (1974).

6. *Lewis v. New Orleans*, 415 U.S. 130 (1974). See also *Karlan v. City of Cincinnati*, 416 U.S. 924 (1974).

7. *City of Houston, Texas v. Hill*, 482 U.S. 451 (1987).

8. *Watts v. United States*, 395 U.S. 705 (1969).

9. *Watts v. United States*, 395 U.S. 705 (1969). The Court, though, was more sharply split in *Rankin v. McPherson*, 483 U.S. 378 (1987), holding that a public employee could not be fired for remarking during a private conversation, after hearing of the 1981 assassination attempt on President Ronald Reagan, "If they go for him again, I hope they get him." Dissenting Justice Scalia, joined by Chief Justice Rehnquist and Justices O'Connor and White, contended that such speech conveyed no "public concerns" entitled to First Amendment protection.

10. See *Bachellar v. Maryland*, 397 U.S. 564 (1970) (holding that the First Amendment protects Vietnam War protestors before a hostile audience outside of an Army recruiting station); *Edwards v. South Carolina*, 371 U.S. 229 (1963) (upholding First Amendment rights of protestors in front of a state capitol); and *Gregory v. City of Chicago*, 394 U.S. 111 (1969) (upholding the picketing by black activists outside the home of then Chicago mayor Richard Daley). See also *Cohen v. California*, 403 U.S. 15 (1971), discussed in chapter 2, and the discussion later in this chapter on First Amendment protection for public forums and nonpublic forums in which speech and speech-plus-conduct may be regulated.

11. *Beauharnais v. Illinois*, 343 U.S. 250 (1952).

12. See *Smith v. Collin*, 436 U.S. 953 (1978), in which dissenting Justices Blackmun and Rehnquist underscore that "*Beauharnais* has never been overruled," and *R. A. V. v. City of St. Paul*, 505 U.S. 377 (1992) (discussed in the chapter), citing *Beauharnais* approvingly.

13. *R. A. V. v. City of St. Paul, Minnesota*, 505 U.S. 377 (1992). See also Edward J. Cleary, *Beyond the Burning Cross: The First Amendment and the Landmark R. A. V. Case* (New York: Random House, 1994).

14. *Wisconsin v. Mitchell*, 508 U.S. 476 (1993).

15. *Virginia v. Black*, 538 U.S. 343 (2003).

16. *Watts v. United States*, 395 U.S. 705 (1969).

17. The Court also dealt with the Ku Klux Klan's cross burning in *Brandenburg v. Ohio*, 395 U.S. 444 (1969). But in that case the cross burning itself was not specifically at issue, rather a provocative speech given by a speaker standing in front of the burning cross. As discussed in chapter 1, the Court in *Brandenburg* held that, depending on the circumstances, only the advocacy of "imminent lawless action" falls outside of the scope of the

First Amendment, but mere advocacy of lawlessness and even subversive ideas remains constitutionally protected expression.

18. *Stromberg v. California*, 283 U.S. 359 (1931). See also *Halter v. Nebraska*, 205 U.S. 34 (1907) (prior to federal regulation of desecration of the American flag, the Court upheld under the due process clause the use of the flag in advertisements).

19. *West Virginia State Board of Education v. Barnette*, 319 U.S. 624 (1943), overruling *Minersville School District v. Gobitus*, 310 U.S. 586 (1940).

20. *Wooley v. Maynard*, 430 U.S. 705 (1977).

21. See *Brown v. Louisiana*, 383 U.S. 131 (1966).

22. See, for example, *Kelley v. Johnson*, 425 U.S. 238 (1976) (rejecting a challenge to a regulation of the length of police officers' hair as violation of their right of privacy and protected expressive conduct); *Barnes v. Glen Theatre*, 501 U.S. 560 (1991) (discussed in chapter 2); and *Rumsfeld v. Forum for Academic and Institutional Rights*, 546 U.S. 807 (2006) (rejecting a First Amendment challenge to the American Law School's policy of refusing to permit military recruitment on school grounds because of its nondiscrimination policy against sexual orientation in the military; the Court held that law schools had alternative ways of expressing their position).

23. *Clark v. Community for Creative Non-Violence*, 468 U.S. 288 (1984).

24. *United States v. O'Brien*, 391 U.S. 367 (1968).

25. See *Smith v. Goguen*, 415 U.S. 566 (1974), and *Cowgill v. California*, 396 U.S. 371 (1970) (dismissing an appeal raising the issue of whether the display of a mutilated flag was protected).

26. *Spence v. Washington*, 418 U.S. 405 (1974).

27. *Street v. New York*, 394 U.S. 576 (1969).

28. *Texas v. Johnson*, 491 U.S. 387 (1989).

29. *United States v. Eichman*, 496 U.S. 310 (1990).

30. For a further discussion, see Robert Corn-Revere, *Implementing a Flag-Desecration Amendment to the U.S. Constitution*, First Reports, vol. 6, no. 1 (Washington, D.C.: First Amendment Center, July 2005).

31. See and compare the cases discussed in the chapter and notes 20–22 for this chapter. See also *Giboney v. Empire Storage & Ice Co.*, 336 U.S. 490 (1949) (upholding a state's antitrade restraint as applied to picketing by unions), and *Teamsters Local 695 v. Vogt*, 354 U.S. 284 (1957) (holding that states may enjoin peaceful picketing by union organizers).

32. *Hague v. Committee for Industrial Organization (CIO)*, 307 U.S. 496 (1939).

33. *Edwards v. South Carolina*, 371 U.S. 229 (1963).

34. *Cox v. Louisiana*, 379 U.S. 536 (1965).

35. *Cox v. Louisiana*, 379 U.S. 559 (1965).

36. *Police Department of City of Chicago v. Mosley*, 408 U.S. 92 (1972).

37. *Southeastern Promotions v. Conrad*, 420 U.S. 546 (1975).

38. *Boos v. Barry*, 485 U.S. 312 (1988).

39. *Richmond Newspapers, Inc. v. Virginia*, 448 U.S. 358 (1980).

40. *United States v. Grace*, 461 U.S. 171 (1982).

41. *Board of Airport Commissioners of Los Angeles v. Jews for Jesus*, 482 U.S. 569 (1987).

42. *Chief of the Capitol Police v. Jeanette Rankin Brigade*, 409 U.S. 972 (1972).

43. *Widmar v. Vincent*, 454 U.S. 263 (1981).

44. *Lehman v. City of Shaker Heights*, 418 U.S. 298 (1974).

45. *Adderly v. Florida*, 385 U.S. 39 (1966).

46. *Flower v. United States*, 407 U.S. 197 (1972).

47. *Greer v. Spock*, 424 U.S. 828 (1976).

48. *United States v. Kokinda*, 497 U.S. 720 (1990).

49. *International Society for Krishna Consciousness v. Lee*, 505 U.S. 830 (1992).

50. *Arkansas Educational Television Commission v. Forbes*, 523 U.S. 666 (1998).

51. *United States v. American Library Association*, 539 U.S. 126 (2003).

52. *Pleasant Grove City v. Summum*, 129 S. Ct. 1125 (2009).

53. *Healy v. James*, 408 U.S. 169 (1972).

54. *Rosenberger v. Rector and Visitors of the University of Virginia*, 515 U.S. 819 (1995). However, in *Board of Regents of the University of Wisconsin System v. Southworth*, 529 U.S. 217 (2000), the Court upheld mandatory student activity fees over the First Amendment claims of individual students who objected to portions of their fees going to gay and lesbian organizations.

55. *Papish v. Board of Curators of the University of Missouri*, 410 U.S. 667 (1973).

56. *Zurcher v. The Stanford Daily*, 436 U.S. 547 (1978).

57. *West Virginia State Board of Education v. Barnette*, 319 U.S. 624 (1943) (discussed earlier in the chapter).

58. *Board of Education, Island Trees Union Free School District v. Pico*, 457 U.S. 853 (1985).

59. *Board of Education of the Westside Community Schools v. Mergens*, 496 U.S. 226 (1990). See also *Lamb's Chapel v. Center Moriches Union Free School District*, 508 U.S. 384 (1993), and *Good News Club v. Milford Central School*, 533 U.S. 98 (2001) (holding that when schools establish a limited public forum, they may not deny religious schools access to facilities for after-school meetings).

60. *Keyishian v. Board of Regents*, 385 U.S. 589 (1967).

61. *Tinker v. Des Moines Independent Community School District*, 393 U.S. 503 (1969). See also John Johnson, *The Struggle for Student Rights: Tinker v. Des Moines and the 1960s* (Lawrence: University of Kansas Press, 1997); and, more generally, Jamin Raskin, *We the Students: Supreme Court Decisions for and about Students*, second edition (Washington, D.C.: CQ Press, 2003).

62. *Bethel School District No. 403 v. Fraser*, 478 U.S. 675 (1986).

63. *Hazelwood School District v. Kuhlmeier*, 484 U.S. 260 (1988).

64. *Morse v. Frederick*, 551 U.S. 393 (2007).

65. See and compare *Boim v. Fulton County School District*, 494 F.3d 978 (11th Cir. 2007), and *Wisniewski v. Board of Education of Weedsport Center School District*, 494 F.3d 34 (2d Cir. 2007) (both applying *Tinker*), with *Ponce v. Socorro Independent School District*, 508 F.3d 765 (5th Cir. 2007) (applying *Morse* to student speech not pertaining to drug usage but instead to that advocating violence against homosexual students).

Chapter 6

1. Title 48 U.S. Code, Chapter 3, Section 48. For a history of the law, see Adam Ezra Schulman, "History of Animal-cruelty Law at Issue in *Stevens* Poses Incongruity," First Amendment Center, August 2009. www.first amendmentcenter.org/analysis.aspx?id = 21912 (accessed August 4, 2009).

2. *United States v. Stevens*, 533 F.3d 218 (3d Cir.Pa. 2008).

3. *United States v. Stevens, Reply Brief for the United States*, 8–9 (March 31, 2009).

4. *New York v. Ferber*, 458 U.S. 747 (1982).

5. *United States v. Stevens*, 130 S. Ct. 1577 (2010).

Selected Bibliography

Books

Berns, Walter. *Freedom, Virtue and the First Amendment*. Baton Rouge: Louisiana State University, 1957.

———. *The First Amendment and the Future of American Democracy*. New York: Basic Books, 1976.

Black, Hugo LaFayette. *A Constitutional Faith*. New York: Alfred A. Knopf, 1968.

Blackstone, Sir William. *Commentaries on the Laws of England (1765–1769)*. Vol. 4. Reprint. Chicago: University of Chicago Press, 1979.

Bollinger, Lee C., and Geoffrey R. Stone, eds. *Eternally Vigilant: Free Speech in the Modern Era*. Chicago: University of Chicago Press, 2003.

Cole, David. *Enemy Aliens: Double Standards and Constitutional Freedoms in the War on Terrorism*. New York: The New Press, 2003.

Collins, Ronald K. L., and David M. Skover. *The Death of Discourse*. Second edition. Durham, N.C.: Carolina Academic Press, 2005.

Corn-Revere, Robert. *Implementing a Flag-Desecration Amendment to the U.S. Constitution*. First Reports, vol. 6, no. 1. Washington, D.C.: First Amendment Center, July 2005.

Currie, David P. *The Constitution in the Supreme Court: The Second Century, 1888–1986*. Chicago: University of Chicago Press, 1990.

De Grazia, Edward. *Girls Lean Back Everywhere: The Law of Obscenity and the Assault on Genius*. New York: Random House, 1992.

Dershowitz, Alan. *Blasphemy: How the Religious Right is Hijacking the Declaration of Independence*. New York: Wiley, 2008.

Dooling, Richard. *Blue Streak: Swearing, Free Speech, and Sexual Harassment*. New York: Random House, 1996.

Downs, Donald Alexander. *The New Politics of Pornography*. Chicago: University of Chicago Press, 1989.

Eastland, Terry, ed. *Freedom of Expression in the Supreme Court*. Lanham, Md.: Rowman & Littlefield, 2000.

Emerson, Thomas I. *The System of Freedom of Expression*. New York: Random House, 1970.

Feldman, Stephen M. *Free Expression and Democracy in America: A History*. Chicago: University of Chicago Press, 2008.

Friendly, Fred W. *Minnesota Rag: The Dramatic Story of the Landmark Supreme Court Case That Gave New Meaning to Freedom of the Press*. New York: Random House, 1981.

Graber, Mark A. *Transforming Free Speech: The Ambiguous Legacy of Civil Libertarianism*. Berkeley: University of California Press, 1991.

Greenawalt, Kent. *Fighting Words*. Princeton, N.J.: Princeton University Press, 1996.

Hentoff, Nat. *The First Freedom: The Tumultuous History of Free Speech in America*. New York: Delacorte Press, 1988.

Johnson, John. *The Struggle for Student Rights: Tinker v. Des Moines and the 1960s*. Lawrence: University of Kansas Press, 1997.

Levi, Leonard W. *Blasphemy: Verbal Offense Against the Sacred, from Moses to Salman Rushdie*. Chapel Hill: University of North Carolina Press, 1995.

———. *Emergence of a Free Press*. New York: Oxford University Press, 1985.

———. *Legacy of Suppression: Freedom of Speech and Press in Early American History*. Cambridge, Mass.: Belknap Press, 1960.

Levi, Lili. *The FCC's Regulation of Indecency*. First Reports, vol. 7, no. 1. Washington, D.C.: First Amendment Center, April 2008.

Lewis, Anthony. *Freedom of Thought We Hate: A Biography of the First Amendment*. New York: Basic Books, 2010.

———. *Make No Law: The Sullivan Case and the First Amendment*. New York: Random House, 1991.

MacKinnon, Catharine. *Only Words*. Cambridge, Mass.: Harvard University Press, 1993.

MacKinnon, Catharine, and Andrea Dworkin, eds. *In Harm's Way: The Pornography Civil Rights Hearings*. Cambridge, Mass.: Harvard University Press, 1998.

Matsuda, Mari J., et. al. *Words That Wound: Critical Race Theory, Assaultive Speech, and the First Amendment*. Boulder, Colo.: Westview Press, 1993.

Meiklejohn, Alexander. *Political Freedom*. New York: Harper and Row, 1948.

———. "The First Amendment is an Absolute." In *The Supreme Court Review*, edited by Philip Kurland, 245–66. Chicago: University of Chicago Press, 1961.

Miller, John C. *Crisis in Freedom: The Alien and Sedition Acts*. Boston: Little, Brown, 1951.

O'Brien, David M. *Constitutional Law and Politics, Vol. 2: Civil Rights and Civil Liberties*. Seventh edition. New York: W. W. Norton, 2007.

Polenberg, Richard. *Fighting Faiths: The Abrams Case, the Supreme Court, and Free Speech*. New York: Viking Press, 1987.

Raskin, Jamin H. *We the Students: Supreme Court Decisions for and about Students*. Second edition. Washington, D.C.: CQ Press, 2003.

Schauer, Frederick. *Free Speech: A Philosophical Enquiry*. New York: Cambridge University Press, 1982.

Smith, James Morton. *Freedom's Fetters: The Alien and Sedition Laws and American Civil Liberties*. Ithaca, N.Y.: Cornell University Press, 1956.

Smolla, Rodney. *Free Speech in an Open Society*. New York: Knopf, 1992.

———. *Jerry Falwell v. Larry Flynt: The First Amendment on Trial*. New York: St. Martin's Press, 1988.

Stone, Geoffrey R. *Perilous Times: Free Speech in Wartime from the Espionage Act of 1798 to the War on Terrorism*. New York: W. W. Norton, 2004.

Strong, Frank. "Fifty Years of 'Clear and Present Danger.'" In *The Supreme Court Review*, edited by Philip Kurland, 427–80. Chicago: University of Chicago Press, 1969.

Strossen, Nadine. *Defending Pornography: Free Speech, Sex, and the Fight for Women's Rights*. New York: New York University Press, 2000.

Wittern-Keller, Laura, and Raymond Haberski. *The Miracle Case: Film Censorship and the Supreme Court*. Lawrence: University of Kansas Press, 2008.

Scholarly Articles: Law Review and Journals

Alfange, Dean, Jr. "The Balancing of Interest in Free Speech Cases: In Defense of an Abused Doctrine." *Law in Transition Quarterly* 2 (1965): 35–49.

Brennan, William J., Jr. "The Supreme Court and the Meiklejohn Interpretation of the First Amendment." *Harvard Law Review* 79 (1965): 1–20.

Cahn, Edmund. "Justice Black and the First Amendment 'Absolutes': A Public Interview." *New York University Law Review* 37 (1962): 549–63.

Collins, Ronald K. L. "Foreword: To America's Tomorrow—Commerce, Communication, and the Future of Free Speech." *Loyola of Los Angeles Law Review* 41 (2007): 33–37.

Emerson, Thomas I. "Toward a General Theory of the First Amendment." *Yale Law Journal* 72 (1963): 877–956.

Gard, Stephen W. "Fighting Words as Free Speech." *Washington University Law Quarterly* 58 (1980): 531–89.

Hudson, David L., Jr. "Curses! Blasphemy, Profanity Laws Still on the Books." First Amendment Center, 2009. www.firstamendmentcenter.org/analysis.aspx?id = 21938 (accessed September 8, 2009).

McKay, Robert. "The Preference for Freedom." *New York University Law Review* 34 (1959): 1182–1213.

Mendelson, Wallace. "On the Meaning of the First Amendment: Absolutes in the Balance." *California Law Review* 50 (1962): 821–53.

Schauer, Frederick. "The Boundaries of the First Amendment: A Preliminary Exploration of Constitutional Salience." *Harvard Law Review* 117 (2004): 1765–68.

———. "Categories and the First Amendment: A Play in Three Acts," *Vanderbilt Law Review* 34 (1981): 225–30.

Schlag, Pierre. "An Attack on Categorical Approaches to Freedom of Speech." *UCLA Law Review* 30 (1983): 671–713.

Schulman, Ezra. "History of Animal-Cruelty Law at Issue in Stevens Poses Incongruity." First Amendment Center, August 2009. www.firstamendmentcenter.org/analysis.aspx?id = 21912 (accessed August 4, 2009).

Index

About the Author

David M. O'Brien is the Leone Reaves and George W. Spicer Professor at the University of Virginia. He was a judicial fellow and research associate at the Supreme Court of the United States, and held Fulbright teaching and research awards at Oxford University, England; the University of Bologna, Italy; and in Japan. O'Brien was also a visiting fellow at the Russell Sage Foundation in New York, and a visiting professor at Institut d'Etudes Politique Universite Lumiere-Lyon 2, France. He is currently a commissioner on the U.S.-Japan Conference on Cultural and Educational Exchange and the Japan-U.S. Friendship Commission. He is the author of numerous books and articles, including *Storm Center: The Supreme Court in American Politics*, eighth edition, which received the ABA's Silver Gavel Award; a two-volume casebook, *Constitutional Law and Politics*, seventh edition; an annual *Supreme Court Watch*; *Animal Sacrifice and Religious Freedom: The Church of the Lukumi Babalu Aye v. City of Hialeah*; *To Dream of Dreams: Religious Freedom and Constitutional Politics in Postwar Japan*; *Judicial Roulette*; *What Process Is Due? Courts and Science Policy Disputes*; *The Public's Right to Know: The Supreme Court and the First Amendment*; and *Privacy, Law, and Public Policy*. In addition to over one hundred articles and reviews, O'Brien has edited several books and coauthored others, including *Judges on Judging: Views from the Bench,* third edition; *The Lanahan Readings on Civil Rights and Civil Liberties,* third edition; *Abortion and American Politics; Government by the People; Courts and Judicial Policymaking;* and *Judicial Independence: Critical Perspectives from around the World.*

Breinigsville, PA USA
01 August 2010
242805BV00001B/2/P